The

# Superfood
# Diet

low calorie | full flavour | recipes for life

## GURPAREET BAINS

# For a new generation of healthy gastronauts.

First published in Great Britain
in 2014 by Absolute Press,
an imprint of
Bloomsbury Publishing Plc

**Absolute Press**
Scarborough House
29 James Street West
Bath BA1 2BT
**Phone** 44 (0) 1225 316013
**Fax** 44 (0) 1225 445836
**E-mail** office@absolutepress.co.uk
**Website** www.absolutepress.co.uk

**Text copyright**
© Gurpareet Bains, 2014
**This edition copyright**
© Absolute Press, 2014
**Photography copyright**
© Lara Holmes

**Publisher**
Jon Croft
**Commissioning Editor**
Meg Avent
**Art Direction and Design**
Matt Inwood
**Project Editor**
Alice Gibbs
**Editor**
Diana Artley
**Photography**
Lara Holmes
**Food Styling**
Kate Calder

ISBN: 9781472905659

Printed and bound in China by C&C
Offset Printing Co.

**A note about the text**
This book is set in Helvetica Neue.
Helvetica was designed in 1957 by
Max Miedinger of the Swiss-based
Haas foundry. In the early 1980s,
Linotype redrew the entire Helvetica
family. The result was Helvetica
Neue.

**Bloomsbury Publishing Plc**
50 Bedford Square
London WC1B 3DP
www.bloomsbury.com

| Falkirk Council | |
|---|---|
| | |
| **Askews & Holts** | 2014 |
| 641.5 | £14.99 |
| | |

Cover image: Peach, Fig and Crispy Serrano Ham Salad with Orange
Blossom and Ginger Dressing, page 100

Picture opposite: Poached Egg with Fresh Basil and Parmesan, page 54

# The Superfood Diet

low calorie | full flavour | recipes for life

GURPAREET BAINS

Mozzarella, Plum Tomato and Basil on Rye, page 83

# Contents

# My Journey

I never expected that I would find writing a foreword so challenging. For days on end I have endured thoughts that take shape in my head as many contradictory voices. I have been pacing up and down, making tea, washing my hands and doing just about anything at all other than writing. With hindsight, had I known that one day I would air my laundry so publicly, perhaps I might have reconsidered going ahead with this book. But I could not see into the future then, and even now I am not sure where the journey will take me next, and whether one day I will regret my choice.

Although it is at odds with both my British reserve and my Indian wisdom, my heart tells me that this is a path I must now tread, with skeleton in tow. If, by writing this foreword, I can inspire just one individual to become their better self, then it will all have been worthwhile.

As a young child growing up, I was very slim. I was not especially sporty, but neither was I inactive. I remember that I liked to read. I loved to cook. My mother tells me that ever since I was a toddler, I could be found banging away in the kitchen with saucepans, and quite often covered from head to toe in flour.

It was not until my teens that I started piling on the weight. At the time it seemed as if it happened all of a sudden. One day I was slim and then almost overnight I grew into a fatty. At least, that is how it looks in the old photos. But thinking back now, with a degree of introspection, it was not that simple. Nothing ever is. There are layers, even in things that appear uncomplicated.

I do not recall home being a particularly happy place. I had my fair shares of woes, suffering the fallout of my parents' increasingly toxic relationship. This in turn was fuelled by an affliction that affects countless families – my father's own relationship with alcohol.

From my adolescent years, my parents started working harder than ever before to provide for my siblings and me. Early in the morning, after preparing breakfast for us, they would leave the house and I would be left on my own, with more freedom than I had ever had before.  This is when I started eating to gain weight. The larder was well stocked, and I chose to exercise my newly found independence by eating to comfort myself.

As a rotund teen who wore glasses and went to school in a predominantly white area I was up for grabs for the bullies. I do not remember a day at school when I was not bullied or picked on.

The bullying did not only happen at school, however. There was plenty of it at home too, and even more when I was with my extended family in India. Aunts in particular would taunt me, for in a martial race it is dishonourable to be fat. In their eyes, I brought shame upon the family. This miserable state of affairs only led to me eating more. I was not losing weight, certainly. I was getting bigger and bigger.

It was in my late teens that I became fully aware of my weight issue and of how it was limiting my opportunities in life. When you are overweight, you are a fat person first and foremost. Everything else seems to come second. At least, this is how it felt to me. I mean, who really wants to date a chubby boy? This was all the realisation that I needed to propel me to the start of my lifelong weight-loss journey.

By around the age of 16, I was following an unreasonably low-calorie diet, aided by light exercise and appetite suppressants, happily prescribed by concerned healthcare professionals. With this regime, my juvenile and malleable body quickly lost its excess weight. Just as when I gained weight so rapidly in adolescence, it seemed as if I went from fat to fit almost overnight.

I kept the excess weight off for a good few years but, over time, it crept back again. It was inevitable. I had not fully embraced the ethos of healthy eating and exercise. From my early to mid-twenties my weight fluctuated, but always on the heavy side.

By now I had tried a low-calorie meal plan where, although I enjoyed many of the meals, I quickly became frustrated with only 1,600 calories to eat, day in day out. It almost felt like being incarcerated in a gaol of my own making. I know it sounds ridiculous, but this just did not work with my lifestyle. A diet rich in protein and low in sugars has its advantages, such as suppressing appetite, but that works only up to a point. Before long I would confide my feelings in a big bowl of pasta carbonara or some other murderous takeaway. At my peak and, after a night's drinking, it became the norm to find last night's pizza delivery still sitting out on the porch. By now I was topping the scales at a debilitating 110kg.

When I was dieting, I felt controlled and hungry at all times. If I had a few drinks, I would get drunk like a bat out of hell, as my stomach was habitually empty of food. My resolve would crack and I would launch into an eating frenzy that might last for days. I became trapped in a demoralising chain of dieting, binge eating and alcohol abuse where each demon was feeding off the other until I was living my very own hell.

This had become the pattern of my adult life, and I accepted it. I felt weak. I did not know any better. Finding my way out of this complicated labyrinth seemed a vain hope. But nothing is impossible. If you knock on enough doors, soon enough one will open. By my mid-thirties, I stumbled upon insight and gradually broke the cycle that had plagued me for most of my life. Exploring ancient Indian texts, I discovered that in a bygone era regular detoxing was once a routine way of losing excess weight. What I learned was consistent with today's popular 5:2 diet, but there was much more to it than that.

Spices were now recognised as potential weight-loss aids, for their ability to speed up body metabolism as well as to suppress appetite. Even the UK Food Standards Agency endorsed many of the health claims pertaining to spices.

Inspired by these discoveries, I set about creating a diet tailored to my lifestyle. On one day, I would eat freely (within reason); on the next, I would detox by taking in only 600 calories. But on my detox days, I would allow myself to add extra calories to the basic 600, as a trade-off for those I had burned during the day's physical activities.

A typical day for me would involve an hour's walking, as well as a visit to the gym for a 40-minute session on the cardio-wave machine. As well as burning energy, exercise pumped my body full of feel-good endorphins (which in turn meant that I was much more likely to stick to my plan). My total calorie expenditure from physical activity would be around 1,000 calories for the day. So, even on my detox day, I would eat around 1,600 calories. This would alternate with a weight-maintenance day, when I could eat more or less what I liked.

Switching between 1,600 calories to approximately 3,500 the next day did not feel like any diet I had followed previously. In fact, it did not feel as if I were on a diet at all. It was just that I was not binging all the time. Meals were enhanced with herbs and spices, to harness their natural antioxidising, appetite-suppressing and fat-metabolising properties – and they tasted great.

My plan allowed me to do all the things I love most, including eating, exercising and even drinking alcohol occasionally, and all the while losing weight.

On my way up (or down, depending on your perspective) I shed nearly 30kg, and in a manner that was relatively pain-free for me.

**Gurpareet Bains**
London January 2014

# Introduction

Having battled to control my weight from my early teens,
I have been a serial dieter for much of my life. There is no
diet that I have not tried. It has been onwards and upwards
for me as I have watched, year after year and in sheer
terror, the needle on the scales edging up relentlessly, like
a meter in a black cab. I can even recall times in my teens
when I was dragged on to the scales against my will –
kicking, screaming and crying, like a frightened bull.

After many years, I have finally come off the merry-go-
round – leaving behind 30kg and, with it, the traditional
formula for dieting.

Accordingly, I am not about to propose a conventional
diet because, as we know, they just do not work in the
long term. Besides, who really wants to lose weight by
restricting calories for an indefinite period? Or how about
cutting back on carbohydrates to lose weight and therefore
going without our favourite foods? How long do these diets
last before we snap under their impossible demands? Who
can honestly put their hand up and say, 'Put me on a diet'?
Not many of us would wish a diet even on our enemies, so
why do it to ourselves?

# Introduction

If we reflect for just a moment, it becomes clear that our daily lives are spinning at the impossible pace of a washing machine completing its cycle. All around us are fast-moving technological and economic changes. We do not have much time for anything other than work, checking emails, and social media websites. We are becoming less and less mobile. It is our electronic devices that are roaming, not us. Food, especially junk food, is readily available. Our natural equilibrium is out of kilter, and it is our bodies that are paying the price.

We now have on our hands an epidemic of obesity, a condition that was uncommon before the 20th century. The latest data from the Health Survey for England shows that, in 2009, 61.3 per cent of adults were overweight, of whom 23 per cent were obese – a staggering escalation of 17 per cent since the 1980s. Consequently, obesity-related problems such as high blood pressure, high blood cholesterol, type 2 diabetes, heart disease, stroke, certain cancers, gout, osteoarthritis, poor reproductive health and psychological disorders are also on the increase.

Why is it that, as a society obsessed with staying healthy and losing weight, we are becoming fatter and fatter, and increasingly unfit? As I wrestled with this conundrum, I decided that it was time to go searching for answers. And what better place to look than my own Indian heritage? I chose for my starting point one of the world's oldest systems of medicine, Ayurveda, which originated in the Indian subcontinent some 3,000 years ago. Roughly translating into English as 'the science of life', Ayurveda is enshrined in the Vedas, the four ancient texts of Indian knowledge, wisdom and culture. It was one of these texts, the Atharvaveda, which interested me most. It is the oldest known record of medicines and contains over 100 formulations for the treatment of ailments, many of which call for spices as an antidote. The Atharvaveda contains this simple pearl of wisdom, still relevant to us today: 'One should strive to maintain good health by taking a balanced diet and exercising regularly.'

Elsewhere in the Vedas we find regular detoxing extolled, as a means of purifying the body. However this is not a detox as we know it. A Vedic detox would usually entail eating lightly for a period of no more than 24 hours. It was never about starvation. The body was given a chance to repair itself. Equilibrium was restored. Another highly influential work was the Sushruta Samhita, attributed to Sushruta, an Indian surgeon living in the 6th century BC. As well as giving details of more than 300 surgical procedures, it describes more than 1,100 illnesses and 700 medicinal plants. Not surprisingly, much of its content has informed our own medical practice. Ayurveda is at the root of modern medicine.

The second great exponent of Ayurveda, born around 300 BC, was Charaka, the first physician to write about digestion, metabolism and immunity. In the Charaka Samhita he claimed that, 'A man who eats beneficial food is always happy and never suffers from health ailments. He can live for 100 years.' He was not far from the truth, for it is now accepted that those of us who exercise, eat healthily and detox regularly, generally outlive our counterparts.

The Sushruta Samhita and the Charaka Samhita would remain influential for over two millennia. Both texts were translated into Arabic in the 8th century, eventually making their way to Europe.

Another health discipline with its roots in the past is structured exercise. There is nothing new about working out, as we learn from artefacts discovered at the Indus Valley archaeological sites, portraying figures in yogic poses. It appears that yoga was all the rage in Bronze Age India. Perhaps our early ancestors had already discovered the secret of physical, mental and spiritual well-being. At Mohenjo-daro, a great public bath was excavated, which suggests that bathing may have formed part of a fitness regime. In the ancient world, it is possible that the connection between weight control and extended lifespan may have been well understood.

However, there was one more key ingredient to the Ayurvedic model of healthy exercise, sensible eating and detoxification. Spices were carefully employed to control weight and suppress appetite. In recent times, we have lost this wisdom, instead relying on drugs – which, paradoxically, often derive from spices.

Scientists today continue to scrutinise the Ayurvedic system, rejecting some aspects and approving others. The UK Food Standards Agency has recognised the health properties of cinnamon, confirming that just one gram of this spice helps to regulate blood sugar and control appetite. Further afield in Japan, scientists at Tokyo University of Marine Science and Technology have found that fenugreek seeds can be used to help reverse weight gain.

However, for the most wide-ranging research on spices, including their positive impact on health, we must look to the United States Department of Agriculture (USDA). Scientists there have published findings which prove spices to be among the most antioxidising of all available foods. Perhaps the most astonishing discovery was that cinnamon contains 130 times more antioxidants than an equal weight of grapes. This means that, if we choose to incorporate spices like cinnamon into our diet on a daily basis, we can pump our bodies full of antioxidants – with all their beneficial anti-ageing and disease-fighting properties.

The Ayurvedic emphasis on physical activity needs little endorsement from modern medical science. We all know that exercise enhances fitness and well-being, as well as being crucial to a healthy weight-loss regime. However, scientists now have a clearer understanding of the many ways in which regular exercise impacts on the body. Not only does it boost the immune system and help to prevent heart disease, type 2 diabetes and certain cancers, it is also recommended for good mental health and for the alleviation of depression.

Also widely accepted by modern medical science, for its health benefits, is the Ayurvedic principle of detoxification. When we restrict our intake of calories, the body burns sugar stores, known as glycogen, and activates a gene known as SIRT1. This gene in turn metabolises fat to feed the body, and also helps to combat free-radical damage linked to those age-related diseases I have just mentioned. Thus, by detoxing regularly, we can hope to achieve not only weight loss, but also longevity.

My Superfood Diet is about weight loss and lifespan. It is a collection of favourite recipes, deconstructed and reworked until low in calories and fat, and high in antioxidants. To lose weight, we also need to detox every other day. This in turn stimulates our SIRT1 gene, which responds by burning fat and fighting disease. Exercise is the third and final part of the plan: the calories we burn off during physical activity can be traded for more food.

This is a diet that you control almost entirely. Just as with a car, you can push down the accelerator to go faster – in this case, by reducing calories on non-detox days. Lift your foot off that accelerator and the plan reverts to a collection of healthy recipes, high in antioxidants. Many of these antioxidants are provided by spices, which also work to suppress appetite and regulate body metabolism. It is a winning formula, drawing on the ancient wisdom of Indian Ayurveda, backed up by a vast body of recent scientific research, and motivated by my deeply rooted desire not to diet at all.

# The Superfood Diet Weight-loss Programmes

The underpinning formula of the Superfood Diet weight-loss plan is to restrict calorie intake on alternate days, thus creating a calorie deficit which leads to weight loss. A unique feature of the formula is that you can choose from three different plans, depending on what suits your lifestyle best.

The Basic Weight-loss Plan alternates 500/600-calorie detox days with 2,000/2,500-calorie weight-maintenance days.

The next choice is the Flexi Weight-loss plan. You still have a basic allowance of 500/600 calories on detox days, and 2,000/2,500 calories on weight-maintenance days. However, you are permitted to exchange calories burned during exercise for more food. Your personal calorie intake is always of your choosing. How much you eat on a detox or weight-maintenance day is entirely up to you.

The third option is the Express Weight-loss Plan. This allows you to lose a little more weight than the others, by further limiting the calories you can take in on the non-detox days. This plan is not recommended for those who are not physically active.

All three plans are interchangeable. If, for example, you are on the Basic Weight-loss Plan and fancy a workout, you can exchange the calories you burn for more food. Likewise, if you are on the Flexi Weight-loss or the Express Weight-loss Plans and do not feel like going to the gym, or perhaps you are having a lazy Sunday, you can switch back to the Basic Weight-loss Plan. You just need to make sure that you always stick to a detox or weight-maintenance/diet day, but within the rules of the new plan.

Regardless of which of the three plans you choose, you will be alternating detox and weight-maintenance/diet days, which means cycling calorie intake up and down, rather than restricting at the same level each day, as in a traditional diet. For this reason alone, you should avoid the danger of falling into starvation mode.

There is also a wealth of evidence to suggest that calorie restriction switches on the SIRT1 gene referred to earlier. Endocrinologists at Kanazawa Medical University in Japan put obese men on a calorie-restricted diet. After seven weeks, body weight, body mass index, body fat, volatile fatty acids, mean blood pressure and level of fasting insulin all significantly decreased, while maximal oxygen uptake increased. The conclusion was that a calorie-restriction diet is beneficial for obesity-related disorders and induces cellular adaptations against ageing, most likely through SIRT1.

# 1. The Basic Weight-loss Plan

Lose 0.5-1kg per week by alternating a detox day and weight-maintenance day until you arrive at your goal weight. On a detox day, women are permitted 500 calories, while for men it is 600. This is alternated with a weight-maintenance day, when women are allowed 2,000 calories, while for men it is 2,500.

Here, then, is your daily calorie allowance without physical activity:

## Daily calorie allowance without exercise

| Alternating days | Female | Male |
|---|---|---|
| Detox day | 500 | 600 |
| Weight-maintenance day | 2000 | 2500 |

# The Superfood Diet Weight-loss Programmes

## 2. Flexi Weight-loss Plan

If, like me, you would prefer not to diet at all, you simply need to be more active. You can lose 0.5-1kg per week, by combining exercise with alternating detox and weight-maintenance days, until you reach your target weight.

Just as on the Basic Weight-loss Plan, the core allowance on a detox day is 500 calories for women, 600 for men. This is alternated on the weight-maintenance days with 2,000 calories for women, 2,500 for men.

However, with the Flexi Weight-loss plan, the calories you burn during exercise can be exchanged for food. This means that if you walk briskly to work and back, and it takes you one hour, you could earn an extra 300 calories. Add a 30-minute cardio gym session, and you have earned a further 300 calories.

Those extra 600 calories will give women a food allowance of 1,100 calories for detox days, while for men it is 1,200. On the alternating weight-maintenance days, burning off 600 calories translates into 2,600 calories for women, while for men it is 3,100.

Losing weight does not have to be restrictive: you just need to move. There is no limit to the number of calories burned from exercise that can be exchanged for food. The more you move, the more you get to eat, and the further away you are from a traditional diet.

Here is what your calorie intake might look like if you were to burn 600 or 1,000 calories per day exercising, and exchange them for a bigger food allowance:

### Daily calorie allowance with extra 600 calories for exercise

| Alternating days | Female | Male |
| --- | --- | --- |
| Detox day | 1100 | 1200 |
| Weight-maintenance day | 2600 | 3100 |

### Daily calorie allowance with extra 1,000 calories for exercise

| Alternating days | Female | Male |
| --- | --- | --- |
| Detox day | 1500 | 1600 |
| Weight-maintenance day | 3000 | 3500 |

# 3. Express Weight-loss Plan

If you want to go hardcore and lose 1-1.2kg per week, you can further restrict your calorie intake on non-detox days to 1,200 calories for women, 1,600 for men, so in effect they become diet days. You still alternate with a core 500 and 600 calories on detox days but, as before, you are permitted to reward yourself with additional calories for those that you have earned through exercise.

Those extra 600 calories will give women a food allowance of 1,100 calories for detox days, while for men it is 1,200. On the alternating diet days, burning off 600 calories translates into 1,800 calories for women, while for men it is 2,200.

Remember, this plan is not recommended for those who are not physically active. But, if you are able to move your body, it hardly looks like any conventional diet.

Here is what your calorie intake might look like if you were to burn 600 or 1,000 calories per day exercising, and exchange them for a bigger food allowance:

## Daily calorie allowance with extra 600 calories for exercise

| Alternating days | Female | Male |
|---|---|---|
| Detox day | 1100 | 1200 |
| Diet day | 1800 | 2200 |

## Daily calorie allowance with extra 1,000 calories for exercise

| Alternating days | Female | Male |
|---|---|---|
| Detox day | 1500 | 1600 |
| Diet day | 2200 | 2600 |

# Exercise and Activity

My personal journey has taught me that losing weight through dieting alone, without exercise, is a battle fought on an empty stomach. Incorporating exercise into your daily routine is an easier option.

Exercise floods the body with feel-good endorphins, which can strengthen your resolve to stick to a healthier lifestyle. It burns calories, meaning that you can eat more. It increases the body's basal metabolic rate (the energy used when resting), which means that, long after a workout, you will still burn extra calories.

Once exercise becomes a habit and you realise how good it makes you feel, not even wild horses will be able to keep you away. I went from being an overweight person who loathed physical activity to someone who now lives for it.

Start exercising for 30 minutes each day, and build up to 1 hour at least. Consider walking as part of your commute to work, and using your lunch break for a quick cardio workout. Together, these are just two ways for you to incinerate up to 1,000 calories, which can then be exchanged for more food.

You can vary the pace from day to day. I would try to include five intensive cardio sessions per week, and for the remaining days at least go for a gentle walk or swim.

Check how much energy your chosen activity uses, by referring to Counting the Calories You Burn (see page 21). Most exercise machines in gyms are equipped with calorie monitors. There are also plenty of apps that will monitor the calories you burn.

## Weigh Day

Keep it consistent. Weigh yourself once a week or once a fortnight, and stick to that pattern. Make sure that you always weigh yourself after a detox day, and preferably first thing in the morning.

It is normal to lose weight one week and not the next. So do not worry if you do not lose weight every week. Regular weigh-ins are important. Not weighing myself in the past was one of my biggest failings. Ignorance is not bliss.

## Keep a Diary

Keeping a diary is equally important, so make sure you follow this routine from the start of your journey. Use the diary to note down what you are eating and how you are feeling. It is a handy reference tool, which will come in useful if you encounter problems further down the track.

## Recipes for Longevity

The Superfood Diet recipes are mainly low-calorie and low-fat remakes of classics (although there are plenty of new ones, too). I have been pioneering healthy recipes for more than five years now, and I am confident that these ones taste even better than their not so healthful predecessors.

Over the years we have heard much about the metabolic properties of herbs and spices, and that is why nearly all the Superfood Diet recipes use plenty of both. Herbs and spices are also one of the best sources of antioxidants available to us, helping to protect us from free-radical damage to cells, and from associated diseases. Even if you choose not to pursue a weight-loss plan, you can still benefit from using healthy recipes that are high in antioxidants. Combined with a sensible lifestyle, they will give you the best possible chance of keeping fit in the long term.

## When Do I Eat?

Eat when you are hungry. If you are not a breakfast person, or you prefer to work out on an empty stomach, eat later. Perhaps you prefer a heavier lunch and a lighter dinner, or vice versa. You choose. Stick within your calorie limitations and you will lose weight.

## What if I Break my Diet?

Just get back on the plan the very next day, at the latest. Keep going and you will get there eventually.

## Hunger Pangs

At the start of any healthy eating regimen, you may experience hunger pangs, especially after exercise – or you may not encounter them at all. Most people can ride these out but, if you do find them unbearable, here are a few tips to help you cope.

Try sipping my Appetite-suppressant Diet Tea (see page 213) throughout the day. It uses cinnamon and fennel to take the edge off your hunger.

Include more protein-rich meals in your diet. Unlike carbohydrates, proteins fill you up without causing a spike in your blood sugar levels – the usual culprit that causes hunger pangs.

When you are hungry, try to use some of the very low-calorie recipes. They can fill you up without filling you out. I usually have a 45- or 50-calorie soup on standby in the refrigerator.

Take advantage of Slim Noodles and Pasta. Made from a vegetable fibre that your body cannot absorb, they contain minimal calories. The fibre slows down the digestive process, which means that you will feel full for a long time after eating.

Try to pinpoint the cause of your hunger pangs. Sometimes it is not as simple as we think. Fatigue, boredom, TV and alcohol can all be triggers. Ensuring that you have enough rest and exercise will alleviate the first two causes. For TV, the only answer is avoidance. For alcohol, the advice is the same, for the following reasons.

## Alcohol

Alcohol is a dieter's worst friend. Not only does it contain empty calories, it can disperse resolve faster than a water cannon disbands a crowd. After a few drinks, it is so easy to indulge in some late-night munching – and this loss of control can extend even to the next day, as you nurse a hangover.

Alcohol is a diuretic, which means that the morning after the night before, you may appear to have lost weight. But within a day or so your weight will creep up again. Slip up regularly and it is unlikely that you will lose any weight. Alcohol is an emotional roller coaster that can break even the most ardent dieter.

Unless you have extraordinary self-control, you are advised to give alcohol a wide berth until you have reached your target weight. I have included a few of my special cocktails in this book, but they are intended only as treats – not recommended for routine indulgence.

## Plateau

When you stop losing weight for a time – usually, for up to three weeks – we call it a plateau. It is a normal occurrence on any diet, and persistence is the key here. However, there are a few things that you can do to keep things moving, and this is where keeping a diary comes in handy.

First, make sure you are weighing yourself after a detox day, and at the same time each day.

# Exercise and Activity

Be honest when counting calories. Account for every single bite you take. Even a small boiled sweet can contain over 40 calories. Inaccuracy here is the most likely cause for not losing weight.

Be equally honest when calculating the calories expended. Exaggerated guesstimates here are the second biggest reason for not losing weight. Try not to cheat when assessing your real level of activity. If you have hit a plateau for three weeks, and have any doubts in this area, I suggest that you bar yourself from earning extra calories from activities that are hard to monitor, such as housework and sex. Stick to accumulating calories from structured exercise only.

Consider building a small weightlifting routine into your fitness programme. Lifting weights that are slightly uncomfortable to hold up, a few times a week, is all it takes. Your body's calorie consumption increases as you grow muscle mass. For weightlifting advice, talk to a fitness instructor at your local gym.

You could also switch to the Express Weight-loss Plan for a week or two, to kick-start your engine.

## Maintenance Plan

At last, you have arrived at your goal weight. Congratulations!

To stop the needle on the scale climbing back up again, you need to stick to a basic food allowance of 2,000 calories per day for a woman, 2,500 for a man. As before, you can top up these allowances with additional calories that you have earned from physical activity. Make sure that you continue to weigh yourself regularly. Just hoping that all is well does not work for most of us. If you do slip up and gain weight, just jump back on to one of the weight-loss plans.

Remember to keep moving. If you can get up a little earlier or spare your lunch break to walk and exercise for at least an hour each day, you are creating a habit of regular physical activity, which you can trade for more food.

This does not have to feel like a diet at all.

# Counting the Calories You Burn

| Activity | Calories burned per hour, according to weight | | |
|---|---|---|---|
| | 70kg | 80kg | 90kg |
| Walking 2 mph | 195 | 220 | 250 |
| Housework | 200 | 230 | 260 |
| Dancing – slow | 215 | 245 | 270 |
| Cycling – slow | 275 | 320 | 355 |
| Sex – intercourse | 300 | 340 | 380 |
| Walking 3 mph | 305 | 350 | 390 |
| Walking 4 mph | 360 | 410 | 465 |
| Gardening | 380 | 435 | 490 |
| Dancing – fast | 390 | 445 | 500 |
| Swimming – moderate | 425 | 490 | 545 |
| Aerobics – low impact | 425 | 490 | 545 |
| Aerobics – high impact | 490 | 560 | 630 |
| Jogging | 490 | 560 | 630 |
| Running 5 mph | 590 | 675 | 760 |
| Cycling 12-14 mph | 610 | 700 | 785 |
| Swimming – vigorous | 685 | 780 | 880 |

# Counting the Calories You Eat

## Fruit and Vegetables (Raw)

| 100g unless specified otherwise | Calories | Fat in grams |
|---|---|---|
| Apple, 1 medium | 82 | 0.6 |
| Asparagus | 20 | 0.1 |
| Aubergine | 25 | 0.2 |
| Avocado | 190 | 19.5 |
| Baby corn | 26 | 0.4 |
| Banana | 89 | 0.3 |
| Beansprouts | 30 | neg |
| Blueberries | 45 | 0.3 |
| Broccoli | 34 | 0.4 |
| Cabbage | 26 | 0.2 |
| Carrot | 30 | 0.3 |
| Celery | 16 | 0.2 |
| Courgette | 17 | 0.3 |
| Cucumber | 10 | 0.1 |
| Dates | 270 | 0.2 |
| Figs | 74 | 0.3 |
| Grapefruit | 42 | 0.1 |
| Grapes | 67 | 0.4 |
| Green peas | 50 | 0.9 |
| Green pepper | 15 | 0.3 |
| Leek | 22 | 0.5 |
| Lettuce | 17 | 0.3 |
| Lime, 1 | 20 | 0.1 |
| Mango | 57 | 0.2 |

| 100g unless specified otherwise | Calories | Fat in grams |
| --- | --- | --- |
| Mango pulp | 97 | 0.4 |
| Marrow | 12 | 0.2 |
| Mushrooms | 16 | 0.5 |
| Nectarine | 39 | 0.2 |
| Okra | 33 | 0.2 |
| Onion | 36 | 0.2 |
| Orange | 47 | 0.1 |
| Parsnip | 75 | 0.3 |
| Passion fruit | 97 | 0.7 |
| Peach | 39 | 0.2 |
| Pear, 1 medium | 60 | 0.1 |
| Pomegranate | 83 | 1.2 |
| Potato | 77 | 0.1 |
| Pumpkin | 13 | 0.2 |
| Raspberries | 53 | 0.6 |
| Red pepper | 30 | 0.6 |
| Runner beans | 21 | neg |
| Samphire | 26 | 0.3 |
| Spinach | 34 | 0.8 |
| Strawberries | 33 | 0.3 |
| Swede | 38 | 0.2 |
| Sweet Potato | 86 | neg |
| Sweetcorn | 80 | 1.1 |
| Tomato, 1 medium | 26 | 0.4 |
| Watermelon | 30 | 0.2 |

# Counting the Calories You Eat

## Rices, Pulses and Grains

| 100g unless specified otherwise | Calories | Fat in grams |
|---|---|---|
| Basmati and wild rice, raw | 349 | 0.4 |
| Basmati rice, raw | 348 | 0.4 |
| Black-eyed beans, canned | 130 | 0.7 |
| Brown lentils, dried | 297 | 1.9 |
| Brown rice, raw | 357 | 2.8 |
| Chickpeas, canned | 164 | 2.6 |
| Flageolet beans, canned | 107 | 0.8 |
| Kidney beans, canned | 95 | 0.6 |
| Pearl barley, raw | 361 | 1.2 |
| Puy lentils, raw | 307 | 1.2 |
| Quinoa, raw | 374 | 5.8 |
| Red lentils, dried | 318 | 1.3 |
| Soya beans, raw | 446 | 20 |
| Sushi rice, raw | 330 | 0.5 |
| Jasmine rice, raw | 388 | 0.8 |

**The Superfood Diet**

# Dairy and Dairy Substitutes (Uncooked)

| 100g unless specified otherwise | Calories | Fat in grams |
|---|---|---|
| Almond milk, unsweetened, 100ml | 13 | 1.1 |
| Cheddar cheese, low-fat | 318 | 21.2 |
| Cottage cheese, low-fat | 83 | 2.2 |
| Feta cheese, low-fat | 182 | 11.5 |
| Greek yogurt, fat-free | 57 | 0.0 |
| Greek yogurt, low-fat | 59 | 2.0 |
| Halloumi cheese, low-fat | 253 | 15.0 |
| Milk, semi-skimmed, 100ml | 49 | 1.7 |
| Mozzarella cheese, low-fat | 176 | 10.5 |
| Natural yogurt, low-fat, 100ml | 58 | 1.7 |
| Parmesan cheese | 415 | 30.0 |
| Quark (skimmed milk soft cheese) | 69 | 0.2 |

# Seafood

| 100g unless specified otherwise | Calories | Fat in grams |
|---|---|---|
| Cod, raw | 80 | 0.7 |
| Prawns, raw | 85 | 0.5 |
| Salmon, raw | 131 | 8.6 |
| Smoked salmon | 142 | 4.5 |
| Tuna in brine, canned | 105 | 0.5 |

# Counting the Calories You Eat

## Meat, Eggs and Tofu

| 100g unless specified otherwise | Calories | Fat in grams |
|---|---|---|
| Beef, lean chuck steak, raw | 140 | 4.0 |
| Beef, extra lean steak mince, raw | 123 | 4.5 |
| Chicken, skinless breast, raw | 114 | 2.5 |
| Egg, 1 medium | 78 | 6.3 |
| Serrano ham | 225 | 11 |
| Smoked ham | 107 | 3 |
| Tofu | 76 | 3.5 |
| Turkey, lean breast meat, raw | 127 | 1 |
| Turkey, lean breast mince, raw | 137 | 2 |
| Turkey, lean thigh mince, raw | 175 | 7.35 |
| Turkey rasher (turkey bacon), grilled, 1 slice | 25 | 0.1 |

## Dried Fruits

| 100g unless specified otherwise | Calories | Fat in grams |
|---|---|---|
| Apricots | 296 | 0.6 |
| Dried mixed fruit | 295 | 1.0 |
| Goji berries | 330 | 1.8 |
| Raisins | 295 | 0.4 |

**The Superfood Diet**

# Nuts

| 100g unless specified otherwise | Calories | Fat in grams |
|---|---|---|
| Almonds, unblanched | 576 | 49.0 |
| Cashew nuts | 584 | 47.0 |
| Peanuts | 564 | 46.0 |
| Pine nuts | 673 | 68.0 |
| Pistachio nuts | 562 | 45.0 |
| Walnuts | 654 | 65.0 |

# Breads

| | Calories | Fat in grams |
|---|---|---|
| Bagel, ½ | 130 | 1.5 |
| Pitta, wholemeal, 1 | 138 | 1.6 |
| Rye, 1 slice | 125 | 1.25 |
| Sourdough, 1 slice | 125 | 0.6 |
| Wholegrain, 1 slice | 100 | 1.9 |
| Wholemeal, 1 slice | 100 | 1.0 |
| Wrap, wholemeal, 1 | 190 | 4.0 |

# Counting the Calories You Eat

## Flour, Cereals and Seeds

| 100g unless specified otherwise | Calories | Fat in grams |
| --- | --- | --- |
| Cornflour, 1 tablespoon | 64.8 | neg |
| Cornmeal (polenta) | 375 | 1.4 |
| Oats, rolled | 374 | 8.0 |
| Pumpkin seeds | 559 | 49.0 |
| Rice flour | 357 | 2.2 |
| Rye flour | 304 | 1.9 |
| Sesame seeds | 630 | 58.0 |
| Spelt flour, white | 342 | 2.0 |
| Spelt flour, wholegrain | 330 | 2.5 |
| Wholemeal flour | 316 | 2.2 |

## Sweeteners

| 1 teaspoon | Calories | Fat in grams |
| --- | --- | --- |
| Agave nectar | 13.6 | 0 |
| Honey | 22 | 0 |
| Sugar | 20 | 0 |

# Fats

| 1 tablespoon | Calories | Fat in grams |
|---|---|---|
| Coconut oil | 135 | 15.0 |
| Mayonnaise, full-fat | 100 | 11.0 |
| Olive oil | 135 | 15.0 |
| Sesame oil | 135 | 15.0 |

# Everything Else

| 100g unless specified otherwise | Calories | Fat in grams |
|---|---|---|
| Cocoa powder | 330 | 21.7 |
| Coconut milk, light, 100ml | 77 | 7.6 |
| Orange juice, 100ml | 40 | 0.1 |
| Passata | 32 | 0.2 |
| Rice paper, 1 x 22 cm diameter | 8 | neg |
| Tomato purée, 1 tablespoon | 15 | neg |

# Antioxidants

## What is an Antioxidant?

Antioxidants help to guard against degeneration and disease. They slow down and prevent the oxidation of free radicals which, if left unhindered, start chain reactions that damage cells. Antioxidants eliminate these potential chain reactions, by removing free-radical transmitters, thus inhibiting cell damage. They can be found in a myriad of foods and spices, and are linked with preventing, and even fighting, cancer, heart disease and type 2 diabetes, in addition to numerous degenerative conditions.

## What are the Best Sources of Antioxidants?

The ORAC value (Oxygen Radical Absorbance Capacity) is the scientific measurement of the antioxidant capacity of foods and spices. It was developed by scientists at the National Institutes of Health in Maryland, USA. Foods higher on the ORAC scale will neutralise free radicals more effectively. The United States Department of Agriculture (USDA), in Washington, DC, publishes ORAC values of both foods and spices. The average person consumes approximately 1,200 ORAC units per day. USDA recommends between 3,000 and 5,000 ORAC units per day for significant antioxidant protection and optimal health.

# ORAC Values of Foods

| Item | ORAC value per 100g | Item | ORAC value per 100g |
|---|---|---|---|
| Acai berries | 102,700 | Leeks | 569 |
| Almonds | 4,454 | Lemon juice | 1,225 |
| Apple | 3,049 | Lentils | 7,282 |
| Apricots, dried | 3,234 | Lettuce, Iceberg | 438 |
| Aubergine | 932 | Lime | 82 |
| Avocado | 1,922 | Lime juice | 1,225 |
| Banana | 795 | Mangetout | 759 |
| Beansprouts | 1,510 | Mango | 1,300 |
| Blueberries | 6,552 | Oats | 1,708 |
| Broccoli | 1,510 | Olive oil | 372 |
| Cabbage, red | 2,496 | Onion, red | 1,521 |
| Cabbage, white | 529 | Onion, white | 863 |
| Carrot | 697 | Orange | 2,103 |
| Cashew nuts | 1,948 | Orange juice | 726 |
| Celery | 552 | Passata | 694 |
| Chickpeas | 847 | Peach | 1,922 |
| Chocolate, dark | 20,816 | Peanuts | 3,166 |
| Cocoa powder | 55,653 | Peas, green | 600 |
| Courgette | 180 | Pepper, green | 935 |
| Cucumber | 232 | Pepper, red | 821 |
| Dates | 3,895 | Pineapple | 385 |
| Figs | 3,383 | Pistachio nuts | 7,675 |
| Goji berries | 3,290 | Pomegranate juice | 2,681 |
| Kidney beans | 8,606 | Popcorn | 1,743 |

# Antioxidants

## ORAC Values of Foods (continued)

| Item | ORAC value per 100g |
| --- | --- |
| Potato | 1,058 |
| Pumpkin | 483 |
| Radishes | 1,750 |
| Raspberries | 5,065 |
| Raisins | 3,406 |
| Rocket | 1,904 |
| Soya beans | 5,764 |
| Spinach | 1,513 |
| Strawberries | 4,302 |
| Sultanas | 3,406 |
| Sweet potato | 902 |
| Sweetcorn, canned | 413 |
| Tea, green, brewed | 1,253 |
| Tomato juice | 486 |
| Tomatoes | 546 |
| Walnuts | 13,541 |
| Watermelon | 142 |
| Wine, red | 3,707 |

# ORAC Values of Spices

| Item | ORAC value per 100g | Item | ORAC value per 100g |
|---|---|---|---|
| Basil, fresh | 4,805 | Oregano, dried | 175,295 |
| Black pepper, ground | 34,053 | Paprika | 21,932 |
| Cardamom pods | 2,764 | Parsley, fresh | 1,301 |
| Chilli powder | 23,636 | Rosemary, dried | 165,280 |
| Chives | 2,094 | Sage, fresh | 32,004 |
| Cinnamon, ground | 131,420 | Turmeric | 127,068 |
| Cloves | 290,283 | | |
| Coriander, fresh | 5,141 | | |
| Cumin, seeds | 50,372 | | |
| Curry powder | 48,504 | | |
| Dill, fresh | 4,392 | | |
| Garlic, fresh | 5,708 | | |
| Garlic powder | 6,665 | | |
| Ginger, fresh root | 15,480 | | |
| Ginger, ground | 39,041 | | |
| Mint, fresh | 13,978 | | |
| Mustard seeds | 29,257 | | |
| Nutmeg, ground | 69,640 | | |

# Before You Start

Here are a few pointers on some of the ingredients used, especially the more unusual ones, and a note on portion sizes.

## Agave nectar

You will find agave nectar in most large supermarkets. It is sweeter than honey or sugar, but lower in calories. Agave nectar is almost void of flavour, so cannot generally be substituted for honey.

## Mayonnaise

Choosing not to compromise on taste, I use small amounts of full-fat mayonnaise, rather than the low-fat variety. Often I mix it with yogurt. The aim is for a taste that does not say: diet food.

## Rye bread

I prefer to toast rye bread. Untoasted, the taste is slightly bitter and the texture unappealing. Toast on a low heat setting until deliciously crisp. Because rye is so moist, it takes much longer to toast than other breads.

## Salt

From the health point of view, it is wise to go easy on salt. What type you use and how much – indeed, whether you choose to add salt at all – is a personal choice. My own preference is for coarsely ground sea or rock salt, but a finely ground product is best for baking.

## Samphire

This enchanting vegetable grows near the seashore, which is why the bright green shoots taste slightly of salt. In season during the summer months, it is harder to source in winter - although some larger supermarkets are starting to import it year round. There is no substitute.

## Sea salad

Sea salad is a selection of dried sea vegetables, or seaweeds. It can be purchased online and from some health-food shops and larger supermarkets. If you have difficulty finding it, just omit from the recipe.

## Sushi nori

Nori is one of the edible seaweeds often found in sea salad. Dried, pressed nori is used to wrap Japanese sushi, hence the name, sushi nori. These dark green, papery sheets can be found at larger supermarkets as well as oriental food shops. If unavailable, omit from the recipe.

## Sushi rice

This is the short-grain, slightly sticky rice, used vinegared in Japanese sushi. It is perfect for big eaters and all those with hunger to quell. Because it is super-absorbent, it will fill you up without filling you out.

## Slim Pasta and Noodles

These miracle fillers, made from an unabsorbable vegetable fibre, are almost bereft of calories. Tossed in a salad or soup, they will provide a satisfying meal of less than 100 calories. They do not soak up sauce in the way traditional pasta and noodles do, so take some getting used to when teamed with an Italian pasta sauce. I recommend trying them first in a salad or soup. Because they are one of the most filling foods you will ever eat, take care not to overindulge (at least, until you are familiar with them). They are not cheap but are well worth trying. Find them, and Slim Rice, at all good health-food shops.

## Turkey

You will see a number of turkey-based recipes. Many of you, I know, will think that turkey is just for Christmas, but I have to disagree – especially bearing in mind that turkey contains half the fat of chicken. The trick to creating tasty food is knowing how to prepare it properly. I am sure that turkey meat will become a favourite, if you give it a go. Find it in larger supermarkets.

## Yogurt

I use three types of yogurt in my cooking: low-fat natural, low-fat Greek and fat-free Greek. To ensure good results, always use the type specified. For fat-free, choose Fage Total 0% fat.

## Portion sizes

Some of you may find the portion sizes modest. However, you are not limited by portion size. It is the calorie count that matters. Only you know whether you can have a second portion or not. Big eaters will find plenty of low-calorie recipes where they can enjoy many portions, should they wish to indulge.

All calorie and fat counts are for single portions.

# Breakfast

# At a glance...

**59 Turkey BLT on Toasted Sesame Bagel**

240 kcal/6g fat

**60 Spicy Scrambled Tofu on Toast**

295 kcal/13g fat

**61 Ham and Egg Big Breakfast on Rye**

405 kcal/13.5g fat

# Soft Boiled Egg with Carrot Soldiers

## 80 kcal/6g fat

**Serves 1**

According to studies at Saint Louis University in Missouri, 'an egg breakfast enhances weight loss, when combined with an energy-deficient diet. The inclusion of eggs in a weight-management programme may offer a nutritious supplement to enhance weight loss.' You might also appreciate how the sweet carrot soldiers complement the savoury egg.

**1 egg**
**10 carrot batons**
**a small pinch of chilli powder**
**freshly ground black pepper and**
**    sea salt, to taste**

Place the egg in a small pan of cold water, bring to the boil and simmer for 3 minutes. Place the carrot batons in another small pan, cover with boiling water and simmer for 1 minute.

Remove the egg from the pan and place in an egg cup. Drain the carrot batons, rinse in plenty of cold water, then drain again. Slice the top off the egg. Sprinkle on the chilli, black pepper and salt if using. Serve with the carrot batons as soldiers.

**Chilli**
fat metabolism, metabolism booster
**Black pepper**
fat metabolism, metabolism booster

**Breakfast**

The Superfood Diet

# Mini Thai-style Prawn and Egg Frittatas

115 kcal/6.5g fat

**Serves 6**

Small, yes, yet mighty enough to tackle a hunger whilst simultaneously delivering a colossal wallop of taste. Perfectamundo for a breakfast-on-the-go.

**80g baby spinach leaves, coarsely chopped**
**6 eggs**
**2 tablespoons sweet chilli sauce**
**100g cooked peeled prawns, finely chopped**
**1 red pepper, finely diced**
**1 tablespoon chopped fresh coriander**
**1 teaspoon grated fresh root ginger**
**¼ teaspoon chilli powder (optional)**
**freshly ground black pepper**
**sesame oil**

Preheat the oven to 180°C/fan 160°C/Gas Mark 4. Place the chopped baby spinach leaves in a microwave-safe bowl, cover and microwave on HIGH for about 30 seconds or until the leaves wilt slightly. Carefully remove from the microwave and set aside.

In a large bowl, beat the eggs with the chilli sauce. Mix in the prawns, red pepper, coriander, ginger and chilli powder (if using), and season with black pepper. Fold in the wilted spinach.

Brush a 6 hole muffin tin with a drop of sesame oil. Divide the mixture equally between the muffin cups and bake in the centre of the oven for 25 minutes or until set. Allow to cool and serve at room temperature or chilled.

**Coriander**
diuretic
**Ginger**
diuretic, fat metabolism
**Chilli**
fat metabolism, metabolism booster
**Black pepper**
fat metabolism, metabolism booster

# Nectarines with Yogurt and All-Bran

## 125 kcal/1.5g fat

**Serves 1**

All-Bran is more than 40 per cent fibre, so there are not too many calories to worry about.

**1 nectarine, cored and sliced**
**4 tablespoons low-fat Greek yogurt**
**10g All-Bran cereal**
**1 teaspoon clear honey**
**a pinch of ground cinnamon**

Place the nectarine slices in a small serving bowl. Top with the yogurt, All-Bran, honey and cinnamon.

**Cinnamon**
appetite suppressant, glucose and fat metabolism

# Apricots Poached with Lemongrass

## 150 kcal/0.3g fat

**Serves 4**

A few simple spices can turn the ordinary into the extraordinary.

**200g dried apricots**
**1 stalk of lemongrass, cut into 4
  pieces**
**1 stick of cinnamon**
**2 star anise**
**5 green cardamom pods, lightly
  crushed**
**3 cloves**

Place all the ingredients in a saucepan with 1 litre cold water. Bring to the boil, then reduce the heat to a simmer and cook, uncovered, for 30 minutes, stirring occasionally.

Remove the pan from the heat and allow the mixture to cool, then refrigerate. Serve chilled.

**Cinnamon**
appetite suppressant, glucose and fat metabolism
**Cloves**
fat metabolism

# Red Grapefruit, Honey and Mint Fruit Salad

155 kcal/0.3g fat

**Serves 1**

Scientists from the Scripps Clinic in sunny California tested the effects of grapefruit on weight and insulin resistance. They concluded that 'Half a fresh grapefruit eaten before meals was associated with significant weight loss. Although the mechanism of this weight loss is unknown it would appear reasonable to include grapefruit in a weight-reduction diet.'

**1 red or pink grapefruit, peeled and cut into large chunks**
**2 teaspoons clear honey**
**1 tablespoon chopped fresh mint**
**a pinch of sea salt**

Combine all of the ingredients in a large bowl and serve.

# Breakfast in a Gee Whiz

## 160 kcal/3g fat

**Serves 1**

A perfect on-the-go breakfast of banana, cereal and milk. It is best to use frozen banana pieces here if you want to achieve a deliciously thick and creamy texture.

**100g banana, frozen and cut into pieces**
**10g All-Bran cereal**
**250ml unsweetened almond milk**
**½ teaspoon vanilla extract**
**a pinch of ground cinnamon**
**a large handful of ice, plus extra to serve**

Put all the ingredients into a blender and blend together until smooth.

Place the extra ice in tall glasses and pour in the smoothie. Serve immediately.

**Cinnamon**
appetite suppressant, glucose and fat metabolism

# Lentil and Pearl Barley Breakfast Soup

170 kcal/1g fat

**Serves 7**

Red lentils and pearl barley are ace sources of resistant starch, which are carbohydrates that show an increased fat oxidation in your body after consumption. Now you know how to raise your metabolism by weightlifting a spoon.

**160g red lentils**
**150g pearl barley**
**1 carrot, grated**
**1 chicken or vegetable stock cube, crumbled**
**2 tablespoons tomato purée**
**1 green chilli (optional), chopped**
**1 tablespoon grated fresh root ginger**
**2 teaspoons cumin seeds**
**½ teaspoon fenugreek seeds**
**¾ teaspoon turmeric**
**1 large onion, chopped**
**a handful of green peas (fresh or frozen)**
**lemon wedges to serve**

Place the lentils, barley, carrot, stock cube, tomato purée, chilli if using, ginger, cumin, fenugreek, turmeric and onion into a large pan. Pour in 2 litres boiling water. Place over a high heat and return to the boil, then reduce the heat to low and simmer, uncovered, for 1 hour. Remember to stir frequently to avoid sticking. If the mixture thickens too much, you may need to add a little more boiling water. At the end of cooking the lentils should be cooked to a pulp, and the grains of pearl barley still distinguishable.

Finally, stir in the peas and simmer for a further 3-4 minutes. Serve each bowl of soup with a wedge of lemon on the side, to squeeze in as you like.

**Chilli**
fat metabolism, metabolism booster
**Ginger**
diuretic, fat metabolism
**Fenugreek**
fat metabolism
**Turmeric**
fat metabolism

**The Superfood Diet**

# Mango and Marmite Toast

## 200 kcal/2g fat

**Serves 1**

According to the Japanese, mango and Marmite are umami, a match of savoury with sweet, sour, salty and bitter flavours – and this, say scientists, is what makes food taste irresistible. Umami is strikingly similar to the ancient Ayurvedic concept of a perfect-tasting and health-giving meal, because it is a balance of all these flavours. However, what really matters here is your endorsement.

**1 slice of wholegrain bread**
**Marmite, to taste**
**1 mango, peeled and sliced**
**1 teaspoon agave nectar**
   **(optional)**
**a pinch of ground cinnamon**

Toast the bread, spread with Marmite and top with the mango slices. Drizzle over the agave nectar, if using, and dust with cinnamon.

If mangoes are out of season, try using ripe peaches.

**Cinnamon**
appetite suppressant, glucose and fat metabolism

# Superfoods Pumpkin and Raisin Muffins

## 205 kcal/2g fat

**Makes 6**

These fruity buns have virtually no fat and are sweetened as naturally as possible, so you can rest assured that the muffin top stays firmly on the muffin (and not on you).

**125g white spelt flour**
**60g plain wholemeal flour**
**1¼ teaspoons baking powder**
**1 teaspoon bicarbonate of soda**
**1 teaspoon ground cinnamon**
**½ teaspoon ground nutmeg**
**2 egg whites**
**1 teaspoon vanilla extract**
**600g pumpkin or butternut squash, steamed until cooked, and mashed**
**100g raisins**
**2 teaspoons finely grated fresh root ginger**
**2 teaspoons finely grated lemon rind**
**4 tablespoons agave nectar**
**olive oil**
**15g pumpkin seeds**

Preheat the oven to 200°C/fan 180°C/Gas Mark 6. In a large bowl, combine the flours, baking powder, bicarbonate of soda, cinnamon and nutmeg.

In another bowl, combine the egg whites, vanilla extract, mashed pumpkin or squash, raisins, ginger, lemon rind and agave nectar.

Now combine both the mixtures together. Grease a 6 hole muffin tin with a little olive oil and fill the cups with the mixture equally. Sprinkle over the pumpkin seeds. Bake in the centre of the oven for 20-25 minutes or until the muffins are firm to touch.

**Cinnamon**
appetite suppressant, glucose and fat metabolism
**Ginger**
diuretic, fat metabolism

**Superfood Diet Pumpkin and Raisin Muffin**
205 kcal/2g fat/1735 ORAC units

**Comparable muffin**
422 kcal/19.3g fat/ORAC units neg

# Poached Egg with Fresh Basil and Parmesan

## 210 kcal/8g fat

**Serves 1**

Breakfast fit for a capo di tutti capi (that's a Mafia boss to you or me) who also happens to care about his or her figure.

**white vinegar**
**1 egg**
**1 slice of rye or wholegrain bread**
**a pinch of dried garlic flakes**
**a pinch of chilli powder**
**freshly ground black pepper**
**1 teaspoon grated Parmesan cheese**
**a few fresh basil leaves, coarsely chopped**

Put a couple of sheets of kitchen paper on a dinner plate and set aside.

Bring a large frying pan of water with a drop of white vinegar to the boil. Stir the water with a spoon in a clockwise direction, quickly crack the egg into the water and bring to a gentle simmer. Cook for 3 minutes, then remove the egg with a slotted spoon and leave to drain for a moment on the kitchen paper.

Meanwhile toast the bread. Place the drained egg on the toast. Top with the garlic flakes, chilli powder, black pepper, Parmesan cheese and basil. Serve immediately.

**Chilli**
fat metabolism, metabolism booster
**Black pepper**
fat metabolism, metabolism booster

# Superfoods Dried Fruit, Apple and Goji Porridge

220 kcal/4.5g fat

**Serves 3**

Almond milk is a nutty alternative to dairy milk. It contains approximately one third of the calories found in skimmed milk.

**90g rolled oats**
**50g mixed dried fruit**
**1 apple, peeled and diced**
**½ teaspoon ground ginger**
**500ml unsweetened almond milk**
**1 tablespoon dried goji berries**

Place the oats in a deep, non-stick saucepan. Cook over a medium heat for about 2-3 minutes, stirring frequently, until the oats are roasted. Add the dried fruit, apple and ginger, then pour in the almond milk. Simmer gently, uncovered, for about 2-3 minutes, stirring frequently, until the mixture is soft and mushy.

Mix through the goji berries and serve immediately.

**Ginger**
diuretic, fat metabolism

# Toasted Rye Bread with Fruit and Veg Cottage Cheese Smorgasbord 235 kcal/3g fat

**Serves 1**

Low-fat cottage cheese is a low-calorie, high-protein food, which also makes it rather filling. The trick to mastering a fondness for it is knowing how to pep it up.

**50g low-fat cottage cheese**
**50g cucumber, peeled, deseeded and diced**
**½ tomato, deseeded and diced**
**½ apple, peeled and diced**
**1 date, stoned and diced**
**1 tablespoon chopped fresh chives**
**1 tablespoon chopped fresh dill**
**freshly ground black pepper**
**1 slice of rye bread**

In a small bowl, combine all the ingredients except the rye bread.

Toast the bread, pile the cottage cheese mixture on the toast, and serve.

**Dill**
diuretic, fat metabolism, metabolism booster
**Black pepper**
fat metabolism, metabolism booster

# Omelette Wrap

235 kcal/18g fat

**Serves 1**

Carbohydrates are a treacherous food group. The more we eat, the more we want. Here we outmanoeuvre most of them (or the naughty ones at least).

**1 tablespoon low-fat Greek yogurt**
**1 tablespoon finely chopped fresh chives**
**½ teaspoon mustard seeds**
**1 teaspoon olive oil**
**2 eggs**
**2 teaspoons cold milk**
**freshly ground black pepper and sea salt, to taste**
**½ tomato, deseeded and diced**
**a handful of rocket leaves**
**a small handful of fresh basil leaves**

In a small bowl, combine the yogurt with the chives. Set aside in the refrigerator.

Place the mustard seeds in a non-stick frying pan and cook on a high heat until the seeds start to pop. Remove from the heat and allow the pan to cool for a few minutes. Brush the olive oil evenly over the surface of the pan. Return the pan to heat at a low-medium setting.

Meanwhile, in another small bowl, whisk the eggs with the milk and seasoning to taste.

Once the frying pan is hot, pour in the egg mixture, tilting the pan until the bottom is covered. Leave the omelette to cook for about 1 minute or until set. Turn it over and allow to cook on the other side for 30 seconds. Transfer to a wooden chopping board and allow to cool slightly.

Spread the omelette with the yogurt and chive mixture and sprinkle over the diced tomato, rocket and basil leaves. Fold over the omelette and slice in half.

**Mustard**
fat metabolism
**Black pepper**
fat metabolism, metabolism booster

**The Superfood Diet**

# Turkey BLT on Toasted Sesame Bagel

240 kcal/6g fat

**Serves 1**

Turkey rashers contain one tenth of the fat and one third of the calories of regular bacon. Love at first bite.

**1 tablespoon low-fat Greek yogurt**
**1 teaspoon full-fat mayonnaise**
**1 tablespoon chopped fresh**
   **chives**
**½ sesame bagel**
**½ tomato, thinly sliced**
**2 turkey rashers, cooked**
   **according to packet instructions**
**a handful of rocket leaves**
**freshly ground black pepper**

In a small bowl, combine the yogurt with the mayonnaise and chives, and set aside.

Toast the bagel half, put on a plate and spread with the yogurt mayonnaise mixture. Top with the tomato, turkey and rocket. Season to taste with black pepper and serve.

**Black pepper**
fat metabolism, metabolism booster

**Superfood Diet Turkey BLT on Toasted Sesame Bagel**
240 kcal/6g fat/850 ORAC units

**Comparable BLT**
550 kcal/34g fat/500 ORAC units

# Spicy Scrambled Tofu on Toast

## 295 kcal/13g fat

**Serves 2**

Containing roughly half the amount of fat found in an egg, as well as a load of health benefits, tofu is a menu option well worth exploring. Knowing how to dress it up to make it tasty makes a world of difference.

**1 tablespoon olive oil**
**1 small onion, finely diced**
**1 green pepper, deseeded and finely diced**
**1 green chilli (optional), finely chopped**
**½ teaspoon turmeric**
**2 tomatoes, finely diced**
**1 teaspoon grated fresh root ginger**
**2 teaspoons soy sauce**
**200g firm tofu, crumbled**
**2 slices of wholegrain bread**

Place the olive oil and onion in a non-stick frying pan and cook on a medium heat for about 3-5 minutes or until the onion is soft, stirring frequently. Add the green pepper and chilli, if using, and continue cooking for about 3–5 minutes or until the pepper is slightly softened. Mix in the turmeric and heat for 1 minute.

Add the tomatoes, ginger and soy sauce and cook gently for another 5 minutes or until the tomatoes have softened. Stir in the crumbled tofu, mixing it in thoroughly. Simmer uncovered on a low heat for 5 minutes, stirring frequently.

Toast the bread, spread the spiced tofu mixture on top, and serve.

**Chilli**
fat metabolism, metabolism booster
**Turmeric**
fat metabolism
**Ginger**
diuretic, fat metabolism

# Ham and Egg
# Big Breakfast on Rye

405 kcal/13.5g fat

**Serves 1**

A Northern European-inspired take on our not so healthy classic, bacon and eggs. Perfect for a leisurely weekend brunch.

**1 tablespoon low-fat Greek yogurt**
**1 teaspoon full-fat mayonnaise**
**1 tablespoon finely chopped fresh**
**dill**
**½ tomato, thinly sliced**
**1 teaspoon horseradish sauce**
**½ teaspoon soy sauce**
**2 slices of rye bread**
**1 hard-boiled egg, sliced**
**1 slice of smoked ham**
**a small handful of cress**
**freshly ground black pepper**

In a small bowl, combine the yogurt, mayonnaise and dill and set aside.

In a separate bowl, combine the tomato with the horseradish sauce and soy sauce.

Toast the bread, and put both slices on a plate. Spread the yogurt mixture on one slice and top with the egg. Spread the tomato mixture on the other slice and top with the smoked ham. Garnish both toasts with cress and season to taste with black pepper.

**Dill**
diuretic, fat metabolism, metabolism booster
**Black pepper**
fat metabolism, metabolism booster

**Superfood Diet Ham and Egg Big Breakfast on Rye**
405 kcal/13.5g fat/405 ORAC units

**Comparable English breakfast**
1190 kcal/95g fat/275 ORAC units

# Lunch

# At a glance...

# Cabbage and Pea Ultimate Detox Soup

## 45 kcal/1g fat

**Serves 9**

Made entirely of non-starchy vegetables, you can most certainly afford to ask for seconds, comforted in the knowledge that an Oliver Twist physique is within reach if you so happen to desire it.

**850g white cabbage, quartered and sliced**
**200g carrots, sliced**
**1 onion, sliced**
**1 tomato, quartered**
**2 chicken or vegetable stock cubes, crumbled**
**2 tablespoons mild curry powder**
**50g green peas (fresh or frozen)**
**freshly ground black pepper and sea salt, to taste**

Place all the ingredients except the peas in a large saucepan and cover with 2 litres water. Mix well, and bring to the boil. Reduce to a simmer and cover. Cook for 50 minutes, stirring occasionally.

Remove from the heat and blitz until smooth, adding extra water if necessary. Return to the heat, stir in the peas and simmer for 3-4 minutes. Add seasoning to taste, and serve.

**Chilli (in curry powder)**
fat metabolism, metabolism booster
**Turmeric (in curry powder)**
fat metabolism
**Black pepper**
fat metabolism, metabolism booster

# Superfoods Cream of Oyster Mushroom Soup

50 kcal/1g fat

**Serves 6**

Naturally creamy oyster mushrooms, leek and potato combined with aromatic rosemary means that we don't need to add a smidgen of cream to get a result.

**250g potatoes, peeled and grated**
**1 leek, sliced**
**2 cloves garlic, chopped**
**2 sprigs rosemary**
**½ teaspoon nigella seeds**
**1 chicken stock cube, crumbled**
**1 tablespoon soy sauce**
**350g oyster mushrooms, chopped**
**freshly ground black pepper and**
    **sea salt, to taste**

Place all of the ingredients except the mushrooms and seasoning in a large saucepan and cover with 1.5 litres water. Mix well, and bring to the boil. Reduce to a simmer. Cook uncovered for 15 minutes. Add the chopped mushrooms and continue cooking for another 15 minutes.

Remove from the heat and discard the rosemary sprigs. Blitz the soup until smooth. Season with black pepper and salt to taste.

**Rosemary**
diuretic, fat metabolism
**Black pepper**
fat metabolism, metabolism booster

# Marrow and Quinoa Broth

## 80 kcal/1.5g fat

**Serves 7**

Quinoa contains more protein than any other grain, so now we can enjoy a detox broth that is full of goodness.

1 large onion, diced
1kg marrow, peeled, deseeded
   and chopped
4 carrots, chopped
60g quinoa
1 teaspoon grated fresh root
   ginger
1 tablespoon mild curry powder
2 chicken or vegetable stock
   cubes, crumbled
2 tablespoons each chopped
   fresh mint and dill
freshly ground black pepper and
   sea salt, to taste

Place all the ingredients except the mint, dill and seasoning in a large saucepan and add 1.5 litres water. Bring to a simmer and cook uncovered for 20 minutes.

Remove from the heat and blitz the soup until smooth. Stir in the mint and dill, and season to taste with black pepper and salt.

**Ginger**
diuretic, fat metabolism
**Chilli (in curry powder)**
fat metabolism, metabolism booster
**Turmeric (in curry powder)**
fat metabolism
**Dill**
diuretic, fat metabolism, metabolism booster
**Black pepper**
fat metabolism, metabolism booster

# Cheese Ploughman Sandwich Wraps

## 145 kcal/5g fat

**Serves 4**

A considerable reduction in carbs brings with it a similar curtailment of appetite. Feel free to swap the cheese for prawns or lean roast chicken.

**100g low-fat Cheddar cheese, grated**
**80g Chinese leaf lettuce, finely shredded**
**30g beansprouts**
**1 red pepper, thinly sliced**
**¼ cucumber, peeled, deseeded and thinly sliced**
**½ small red onion, sliced**
**a handful of mint leaves**
**a handful of coriander leaves**
**1 red chilli (optional), deseeded and sliced**
**juice of 1 lime**
**1 teaspoon fish sauce**
**80g sweet pickle or chutney**
**12 x 22cm diameter rice papers (available from oriental food shops)**

In a large bowl, combine the grated cheese, Chinese leaf lettuce, beansprouts, red pepper, cucumber, onion, mint, coriander, red chilli if using, lime juice, fish sauce and sweet pickle or chutney.

Take one rice paper at a time and dip in a bowl of hot water, then place on a wooden chopping board and allow to rest for 1 minute. Place a portion of the filling at the bottom centre of the rice paper. Fold both ends of the rice paper in and roll up firmly.

Repeat with the remaining rice papers until finished. The bowl of hot water needs to be very hot, so you may need to pour in more boiling water as you work.

**Coriander**
diuretic
**Chilli**
fat metabolism, metabolism booster

**3 Superfood Diet Cheese Ploughman Sandwich Wraps**
145 kcal/5g fat/620 ORAC units

**Comparable cheese ploughman sandwich**
430 kcal /22g fat/330 ORAC units

# Hot and Spicy Chicken Nuggets

150 kcal/3g fat

**Serves 3**

Containing hardly any fat, so you can enjoy guilt-free while you banish your bulge back into the space that is known as your subconscious. Try to keep it there. I sure did.

**olive oil**
**400g chicken mini fillets**
**no-salt steak seasoning, to taste**

Preheat the oven to 240°C/fan 220°C/Gas Mark 9. Lightly brush a baking tray with olive oil. Coat the chicken fillets with the steak seasoning, making sure to coat all over.

Place the coated chicken on the baking tray and cook in the centre of the oven for 15 minutes, turning once halfway through.

**Black pepper (in steak seasoning)**
fat metabolism, metabolism booster

**Superfood Diet Hot and Spicy Chicken Nuggets**
150 kcal/3g fat/2300 ORAC units

**Comparable chicken nuggets**
295 kcal/19g fat/ORAC units neg

**The Superfood Diet**

# Chicken Caesar Salad

155 kcal/6.5g fat

**Serves 2**

I have done away with much of the unnecessary fat and carbs – two troublesome food groups to use sparingly. Croutons are replaced with cholesterol-reducing pistachio nuts, which also increase antioxidant levels in your body.

**For the dressing**
**4 tablespoons low-fat Greek yogurt**
**1 teaspoon full-fat mayonnaise**
**1 teaspoon clear honey**
**½ teaspoon curry powder**
**1 tablespoon chopped fresh coriander**
**1 tablespoon chopped fresh dill**
**1 tablespoon chopped fresh mint**
**sea salt, to taste**

**For the salad**
**120g chicken, cooked and sliced**
**140g mixed salad leaves**
**20g pitted green olives**
**½ yellow or red pepper, sliced**
**20g shelled pistachio nuts**

In a bowl, combine the ingredients for the dressing and set aside in the refrigerator.

In a large salad bowl, toss all the salad ingredients except the pistachio nuts with the prepared dressing, then place on 2 serving plates. Garnish with the pistachios and serve immediately.

**Chilli (in curry powder)**
fat metabolism, metabolism booster
**Turmeric (in curry powder)**
fat metabolism
**Coriander**
diuretic
**Dill**
diuretic, fat metabolism, metabolism booster

**Superfood Diet Chicken Caesar Salad**
155 kcal/6.5g fat/1945 ORAC units

**Comparable chicken Caesar salad**
900 kcal/60g fat/545 ORAC units

The Superfood Diet

Left: Prawn and Samphire Balti, page 82
This page: Chicken Caesar Salad, page 73

**The Superfood Diet**

# Turkey Meatloaf

## 170 kcal/4g fat

**Serves 8**

When you learn that lean turkey breast mince contains half the fat of the lowest-fat alternative minced meat, it is a food swap well worth pursuing. Culinary know-how is all it takes to turn ordinary turkey into the extraordinary. For a pronto lunch, take a slice or two to work and team with a tasty salad. Turkey is for life and not just for Christmas.

**500g lean turkey breast mince**
**1 courgette, grated**
**1 medium onion, finely diced**
**3 eggs, lightly beaten**
**90g fresh breadcrumbs**
**65g passata**
**1 teaspoon smoked paprika**
**½ teaspoon chilli flakes**
**20g fresh dill, finely chopped**
**freshly ground black pepper and**
**    sea salt, to taste**

Preheat the oven to 200°C/fan 180°C/Gas Mark 6. Line a baking tray with greaseproof paper.

Place all the ingredients in a large bowl, and knead together until well mixed. Place the turkey mixture on the baking tray and mould into a round loaf shape. Bake in the oven for 1½ hours. Allow to cool before slicing.

**Chilli**
fat metabolism, metabolism booster
**Dill**
diuretic, fat metabolism, metabolism booster
**Black pepper**
fat metabolism, metabolism booster

**Superfood Diet Turkey Meatloaf**
170 kcal/4g fat/435 ORAC units

**Comparable meatloaf**
294 kcal/17.44g fat/200 ORAC units

# Fairy's Thai Red Curry with Poached Cod and Asparagus

## 170 kcal/5.5g fat

**Serves 4**

A Thai curry that contains less calories than an alcopop. I know what I'd rather be having for lunch.

**1 stalk of lemongrass, cut into small pieces and soaked in a little boiling water**
**1 tablespoon red curry paste**
**200ml light coconut milk**
**200g low-fat Greek yogurt**
**1 tablespoon grated fresh root ginger**
**2 cloves garlic, sliced**
**1 teaspoon grated lime rind**
**1 tablespoon fish sauce**
**1 teaspoon sugar**
**4 kaffir lime leaves, sliced**
**a small handful of fresh Thai basil, chopped**
**1 red pepper, diced**
**400g cod fillets, skinned and cut into large chunks**
**100g asparagus, cut into 3cm lengths**

**10g chopped fresh coriander**
**5g chopped fresh mint**

Place the lemongrass pieces, curry paste, coconut milk, yogurt, ginger, garlic, lime rind, fish sauce and sugar in a food processor and blitz until smooth. Pour this mixture into a deep saucepan. Stir in the kaffir lime leaves, basil and red pepper and bring to a simmer over a medium heat. Simmer gently for 10 minutes, uncovered.

Add the cod and asparagus to the pan and return to a simmer. Remove from the heat, cover and leave to stand for 5 minutes so the cod will poach and cook through.

Mix in the coriander and mint and serve.

**Chilli (in currry paste)**
fat metabolism, metabolism booster
**Ginger**
diuretic, fat metabolism
**Coriander**
diuretic

**Superfood Diet Fairy's Thai Red Curry with Poached Cod and Asparagus**
170 kcal/ 5.5g fat

**Comparable Thai red curry**
711 kcal/46g fat

**The Superfood Diet**

# Gluten-free Mediterranean Pasta Salad

170 kcal/12.5g fat

**Serves 2**

Al dente Slim Pasta shines through as the star in this main-course Mediterranean salad.

**For the dressing**
**1 clove garlic, finely chopped**
**2 tablespoons lemon juice**
**1 tablespoon olive oil**

**For the salad**
**200g Slim Pasta penne,**
   **prepared according to packet**
   **instructions, rinsed in cold**
   **water and drained**
**100g mixed salad leaves**
**1 small red onion, sliced**
**10 cherry tomatoes**
**a handful of fresh basil leaves**
**5g pine nuts**
**50g low-fat mozzarella cheese,**
   **diced**
**freshly ground black pepper and**
   **sea salt, to taste**

To make the dressing, put the chopped garlic in a small bowl, add the lemon juice and then whisk in the olive oil. Set aside.

Put all the salad ingredients except the seasoning in a large bowl, add the prepared dressing and toss together. Turn the salad on to 2 serving plates. Season to taste with black pepper and salt and serve immediately.

**Black pepper**
fat metabolism, metabolism booster

# Prawn and Samphire Balti

175 kcal/8.5g fat

**Serves 2**

Samphire is a natural digestive and diuretic used in herbal medicine. These effects are intensified by the spices.

**1 tablespoon light olive oil**
**1 teaspoon mustard seeds**
**½ teaspoon nigella seeds**
**½ teaspoon turmeric**
**½ teaspoon chilli powder**
**200g green prawns**
**100g samphire, washed thoroughly and patted dry on kitchen paper**
**lemon wedges, to serve**

Heat a non-stick wok over a high heat until it is very hot. Pour the olive oil into the wok and heat until the oil is almost smoking – this should take no more than 1 minute.

Add the mustard and nigella seeds and cook until they start to pop – this also should take no longer than 1 minute. Remove from the heat, sprinkle in the turmeric and chilli powder and mix well.

Return the wok to the heat, throw in the prawns and cook for about 2 minutes, stirring frequently, until they have turned white. Mix through the samphire and heat through.

Serve with the lemon wedges.

**Mustard**
fat metabolism
**Turmeric**
fat metabolism
**Chilli**
fat metabolism, metabolism booster

**Superfood Diet Prawn and Samphire Balti**
175 kcal/8.5g fat

**Comparable restaurant Balti**
600 kcal/40g fat

# Mozzarella, Plum Tomato and Basil on Rye

190 kcal/4.5g fat

**Serves 1**

If a sandwich could be a love affair, this one would be Insalata Caprese rendezvousing with Vietnamese Bánh Mì for a one-night stand somewhere in Scandinavia.

**½ plum tomato, sliced**
**30g low-fat mozzarella cheese, sliced**
**1 slice of rye bread**
**1–2 drops sesame oil**
**a few slices of deseeded red chilli**
**a few fresh basil leaves, torn**

Toast the bread. Arrange the tomato and mozzarella cheese slices on top. Shake on the sesame oil and top with the chilli and basil.

**Chilli**
fat metabolism, metabolism booster

# Hummus and Watercress Salad on Wholegrain Toast

190 kcal/5g fat

**Serves 1**

Hummus must be the world's favourite way of eating chickpeas, which are a great source of zinc. This mineral is essential for your body's immune system, and for wound-healing and regulating metabolic rate.

**1 slice of wholegrain bread**
**2 tablespoons Easy Chickpeasy Hummus (see page 165)**
**a few slices of cucumber**
**a few slices of red pepper**
**a small handful of watercress**
**freshly ground black pepper, to taste**

Toast the bread and spread with the hummus. Top with the cucumber, red pepper and watercress. Season to taste with black pepper.

**Chilli**
fat metabolism, metabolism booster
**Coriander**
diuretic
**Black pepper**
fat metabolism, metabolism booster

**The Superfood Diet**

# Prawn and Slim Noodle Salad

210 kcal/10g fat

**Serves 2**

Since Slim Noodles are almost bereft of fat and calories, you can have your fill, yet still allow yourself a wayward pudding.

1 tablespoon sesame oil
½ teaspoon mustard seeds
1 clove garlic, sliced
6 fresh root ginger batons, roughly same size as matchsticks
6 baby corn, sliced in half
1 red pepper, finely sliced
200g Slim Noodles, rinsed and drained
100g baby spinach leaves
150g cooked peeled prawns
10g sesame seeds, toasted
¼ teaspoon asafoetida
1 tablespoon rice vinegar
2 teaspoons mirin
2 teaspoons fish sauce
2 spring onions, finely sliced
½ red chilli, deseeded and sliced
a handful of chopped fresh coriander

Place the sesame oil, mustard seeds, garlic and ginger in a non-stick wok. Heat on a high temperature until the garlic and ginger start to sizzle. Add the baby corn, red pepper and drained noodles and stir-fry for about 3 minutes or until the pepper is softened slightly. Add half of the spinach leaves and mix until they start to wilt – this should take no longer than 1 minute. Turn the noodle and vegetable mixture into a large mixing bowl and allow to cool.

In a small bowl, toss the prawns in the sesame seeds and then tip them into the large bowl of noodles and vegetables. Mix in the asafoetida, vinegar, mirin, fish sauce and remaining spinach.

Place the salad on 2 serving plates and top with the spring onions, chilli and coriander.

**Mustard**
fat metabolism
**Ginger**
diuretic, fat metabolism
**Chilli**
fat metabolism, metabolism booster
**Coriander**
diuretic

# Smoked Salmon with Horseradish and Soy Sauce on Rye

220 kcal/3.5g fat

**Serves 1**

Over a decade of research has shown that if a person eats one portion of oily fish a week, he or she can decrease the chances of dying of a heart attack. Dig in!

**2 teaspoons horseradish sauce**
**½ teaspoon soy sauce**
**1 slice of rye bread**
**a few thin slices of cucumber**
**1 slice of smoked salmon**
**1 teaspoon finely chopped fresh dill**
**a small handful of rocket leaves**

In a small bowl, combine together the horseradish and soy sauce and set aside.

Toast the bread, put on a plate, and spread with the horseradish mixture. Top with the cucumber and smoked salmon, and sprinkle over the dill. Garnish with the rocket leaves.

**Dill**
diuretic, fat metabolism, metabolism booster

# Five-spice Chicken and Avocado on Wholegrain Toast

220 kcal/10g fat

**Serves 1**

Avocados are high in calories, but most of these originate from oleic acid - the monounsaturated fat that is a slow-burning energy source preferred by your body. It is the saturated fats in unhealthy foods which you need to keep a tab on – those are the ones that your body has a tendency to store.

**1 tablespoon low-fat Greek yogurt**
**1 teaspoon full-fat mayonnaise**
**1 slice of wholegrain bread**
**30g cooked chicken, sliced**
**20g avocado, sliced**
**a few drops of soy sauce**
**a pinch of Chinese five-spice**
**  powder**
**1 teaspoon chopped fresh**
**  coriander**
**a few slices of deseeded red chilli**
**  (optional)**

In a small bowl, combine the yogurt and mayonnaise and set aside.

Toast the bread. Put the toast on a plate, and spread it with the yogurt sauce. Top with the chicken, avocado, soy sauce and five-spice powder.

Garnish with coriander and chilli, if using.

**Coriander**
diuretic
**Chilli**
fat metabolism, metabolism booster

**Superfood Diet Five-spice Chicken and Avocado on Wholegrain Toast**
220 kcal/10g fat/435 ORAC units

**Comparable chicken and avocado sandwich**
478 kcal/25.3g fat/385 ORAC units

**The Superfood Diet**

# Superhero's Energising Ham Salad

225 kcal/6.5g fat

**Serves 1**

A salad that consists primarily of low-calorie vegetables and low-fat proteins is a dieter's best friend. I love this salad. Often I put the dressing ingredients in an airtight container in my backpack, and mix it with the salad once I get to my destination. Feel free to swap the ham for lean roast chicken or turkey.

**For the dressing**
**100g low-fat Greek yogurt**
**70g smoked ham, diced**
**½ small red onion, diced**
**juice of ½ lemon**
**2 tablespoons chopped fresh mint**
**2 tablespoons chopped fresh basil**
**½ teaspoon crushed garlic**
**½ green chilli (optional), deseeded and finely chopped**
**freshly ground black pepper, to taste**

**For the salad**
**80g mixed salad leaves**
**100g cherry tomatoes**
**½ small red onion, sliced**
**¼ cucumber, sliced**

In a small bowl, combine the ingredients for the dressing and leave to marinate in the refrigerator for at least 1 hour and up to 8 hours.

Place the salad ingredients in a large salad bowl, add the prepared dressing and toss together.

**Chilli**
fat metabolism, metabolism booster
**Black pepper**
fat metabolism, metabolism booster

# Crispy Serrano Ham on Toasted Sesame Bagel

240 kcal/9g fat

**Serves 1**

Bacon sarnies are an institution for us Brits and I would not want to change that. But I can find ways to please both health nuts and gastronomes.

**1 tablespoon low-fat Greek yogurt**
**1 teaspoon full-fat mayonnaise**
**1 teaspoon chopped fresh dill**
**1 teaspoon chopped fresh mint**
**2 slices of Serrano ham**
**½ sesame bagel**
**a few thin slices of tomato**
**a few thin slices of red onion**
**a handful of rocket leaves**
**freshly ground black pepper, to taste**

In a small bowl, combine the yogurt with the mayonnaise, dill and mint, and set aside.

Grill the Serrano ham until crisp. Toast the bagel half, put on a plate and spread with the yogurt mayonnaise mixture. Top with the tomato and red onion. Finish off with the crispy Serrano ham and rocket. Season with black pepper and serve.

**Dill**
diuretic, fat metabolism, metabolism booster
**Black pepper**
fat metabolism, metabolism booster

**Superfood Diet Crispy Serrano Ham on Toasted Sesame Bagel**
240 kcal/9g fat/1070 ORAC units

**Comparable BLT**
550 kcal/34g fat/500 ORAC units

# Cod, Shiitake and Sushi Rice Stew

## 245 kcal/1.5g fat

**Serves 6**

Shock, horror and dismay. A filling main meal for just 245 calories. The satiating alchemy at work here is the partnering of high-protein, low-calorie cod with water-retaining sushi rice.

1 leek, finely sliced
2 cloves garlic, finely chopped
1 teaspoon finely grated fresh
   root ginger
300g sushi rice
2 carrots, peeled and diced
2 tablespoons miso or 2 chicken
   stock cubes, crumbled
1 tablespoon soy sauce
400g skinless cod fillets, cut into
   chunks
100g shiitake mushrooms, wiped
   and sliced
a large handful of green peas
   (fresh or frozen)
1 tablespoon chopped fresh
   chives
1 tablespoon chopped fresh dill
1 tablespoon chopped fresh mint
white pepper, to taste

Place the leek, garlic, ginger, sushi rice, carrots, miso or stock cubes and soy sauce in a deep saucepan. Cover with 2 litres boiling water and bring to a simmer, stirring a few times to break up any large clumps of rice. Cook on a medium heat, uncovered, for about 15 minutes or until the rice is tender, stirring frequently.

Add the cod, mushrooms and peas to the pan, and bring back to a simmer, stirring. Remove from the heat, cover and leave to stand for 5 minutes so the fish will poach and cook through.

Garnish with the chives, dill and mint. Season to taste with white pepper, and serve.

**Ginger**
diuretic, fat metabolism
**Dill**
diuretic, fat metabolism, metabolism booster

# Stir-fried Tofu with Tenderstem Broccoli

## 250 kcal/13g fat

**Serves 2**

Broccoli is loaded with protein and fibre – both of which are a dieter's best friends. Stir-frying retains both its nutrients and taste. Nothing is worse than boiled broccoli.

1 tablespoon sesame oil
4 cloves garlic, sliced
300g firm tofu, cut into chunks
300g tenderstem broccoli
2 tablespoons fish sauce
1 tablespoon soy sauce
1 tablespoon agave nectar
15g fresh basil leaves
1 red chilli, deseeded and sliced
freshly ground black pepper, to
    taste

Pour the sesame oil into a non-stick wok, add the garlic and heat on a high setting until the garlic sizzles – this should take no more than 1 minute. Add the tofu and broccoli and stir-fry for 5 minutes – you will need to stir frequently.

Add the fish sauce, soy sauce and agave nectar. Heat through, stirring.

Remove from the heat and mix in the basil and chilli. Season with black pepper and serve.

**Chilli**
fat metabolism, metabolism booster
**Black pepper**
fat metabolism, metabolism booster

# Basmati, Wild Rice and Puy Lentil Pilau

300 kcal/3.5g fat

**Serves 4**

Puy lentils are almost one third indigestible fibre, which collects and removes harmful cholesterol from the colon. Cider vinegar enhances this effect.

**½ tablespoon olive oil**
**2 teaspoons cumin seeds**
**2 cloves garlic, sliced**
**100g Puy lentils**
**200g basmati and wild rice**
**2 medium onions, diced**
**1 red chilli, finely chopped**
**1 chicken stock cube, crumbled**
**1 teaspoon ground cinnamon**
**¼ teaspoon ground nutmeg**
**4 tablespoons cider vinegar**
**20g chopped fresh coriander**
**freshly ground black pepper and**
    **sea salt, to taste**

Put the olive oil and cumin seeds in a non-stick frying pan and heat on a medium heat until the seeds start to pop – this should take no longer than 2-3 minutes. Add the garlic and continue cooking for 2 minutes or until the garlic is golden brown, stirring frequently. Remove from the heat.

Turn the cumin seeds and garlic into a large microwave-safe bowl, add all the other ingredients except for the coriander and seasoning, and carefully pour in 500ml boiling water. Mix well with a fork. Microwave, uncovered, for 4 minutes on HIGH at 700W, or for 3½ minutes on HIGH at 800W or for 3 minutes on HIGH at 900W.

Mix again with a fork. Microwave, uncovered, for a further 4 minutes on HIGH at 700W, or for a further 3½ minutes on HIGH at 800W, or for a further 3 minutes on HIGH at 900W.

Mix once more with a fork. Cover the bowl and microwave for a further 4 minutes on HIGH at 700W, or for a further 3½ minutes on HIGH at 800W, or for a further 3 minutes on HIGH at 900W.

Leave to stand, covered, for 10 minutes. Stir in the coriander and black pepper before serving.

**Chilli**
fat metabolism, metabolism booster
**Cinnamon**
appetite suppressant, glucose and fat metabolism
**Coriander**
diuretic
**Black pepper**
fat metabolism, metabolism booster

# Superfoods Gluten-free Turkey and Seaweed Lasagne

## 300 kcal/10g fat

**Serves 6**

I have swapped pasta sheets for rice paper to make this lasagne gluten-free, and lost a considerable amount of calories on the way - and all the while retaining taste. Who needs excess baggage anyway?

**For the meat sauce**
1 tablespoon olive oil
6 green cardamom pods, lightly crushed
1 medium red onion, diced
4 cloves garlic, sliced
1 teaspoon turmeric
500g lean turkey breast mince
100g chestnut or oyster mushrooms, sliced
1 carrot, grated
4 bay leaves
1 teaspoon dried oregano
1 teaspoon smoked paprika
½ teaspoon chilli flakes
15g fresh basil leaves, coarsely chopped
500g passata
sea salt, to taste

**For the cheese sauce**
4½ tablespoons rice flour
700ml unsweetened almond milk
60g low-fat Cheddar cheese, grated
2 tablespoons sea salad or 1 sheet of sushi nori, crumbled (both optional)
15g fresh basil leaves, finely chopped
a pinch of nutmeg

**For completing the lasagne**
9 x 22cm diameter rice papers (available from oriental food shops)
50g grated Parmesan cheese

To make the meat sauce, pour the olive oil into a deep non-stick saucepan, add the cardamoms and cook on a medium heat until the pods begin to sizzle – this should take no more than about 2 minutes. Add the onion and garlic, and fry until the onion starts to soften, stirring regularly – this should take no more than 5 minutes.
Mix through the turmeric and heat through.

Next, add the turkey mince and mushrooms, and cook, stirring frequently, until the meat is sealed – this should take no longer than 5 minutes. Finally, add the grated carrot, bay leaves, oregano, paprika, chilli flakes, basil, passata and salt, and simmer uncovered for 25 minutes, stirring from time to time.

Meanwhile, make the cheese sauce. Place the rice flour in a small non-stick pan and slowly pour in a few drops of the almond milk, stirring all the time until you have a smooth paste. Slowly pour in the remaining almond milk, stirring all the time. Mix in the grated cheese, sea salad or crumbled sushi nori, if using, and the basil and nutmeg. Heat the sauce over a low heat, stirring

regularly. Once it begins to simmer, remove from the heat. Allow to cool, then refrigerate until chilled.

Once the meat sauce has finished simmering, remove from the heat and discard the cardamom pods and bay leaves. Allow to cool, then refrigerate until chilled.

Once the cheese and meat sauces are chilled, preheat the oven to 220°C/fan 200°C/Gas Mark 7. Pour half the chilled meat sauce into a 22cm cake tin, then add a layer of overlapping rice paper (3 sheets per layer). Continue with layers of meat sauce, cheese sauce, and rice paper. Finish with a layer of cheese sauce. Sprinkle with Parmesan cheese.

Bake the lasagne in the centre of the oven for 40 minutes. Remove from the oven and allow to stand for 30 minutes before serving.

**Turmeric**
fat metabolism
**Oregano**
appetite suppressant, fat metabolism
**Chilli**
fat metabolism, metabolism booster

**Superfood Diet Gluten-free Turkey and Seaweed Lasagne**
300 kcal/10g fat/2035 ORAC units

**Comparable lasagne**
702 kcal/49.5g fat/1400 ORAC units

# Superspices Relaxing Beef Masala

## 305 kcal/13g fat

**Serves 4**

In this recipe I use a generous amount of nutmeg that contains the compound, myristicin, which is a natural sedative. Try it one lazy Sunday afternoon, to treat yourself to a soothing end to the week. It is inadvisable to drink alcohol at the same time, and no more than one portion should be eaten in any 24-hour period. It is a recipe for consenting adults only. It is absolutely not suitable for children, the elderly or pregnant and nursing mothers.

2 tablespoons olive oil
20 green cardamom pods, lightly
   crushed
1 tablespoon ground nutmeg
500g lean chuck steak, diced
4 medium onions, finely diced
6 cloves garlic, finely chopped
4 tablespoons grated fresh root
   ginger
2 tablespoons tomato purée
1 teaspoon ground cinnamon
1 teaspoon turmeric
1 teaspoon chilli powder
1 tablespoon soy sauce
2 teaspoons garam masala
25g fresh coriander, chopped

Pour the olive oil into a deep saucepan, add the cardamoms and heat on a medium heat until the pods start to sizzle – this should take no longer than 2-3 minutes. Remove the pan from the heat and mix in the nutmeg. Return the pan to a low heat until the nutmeg starts to sizzle – this should take no longer than 1 minute.

Now add all of the remaining ingredients, except the garam masala and coriander. Pour in 1 litre boiling water and bring back to the boil. Reduce to a low simmer and cook, uncovered, for 2 hours, stirring from time to time. If you need to add water, use 50ml at a time, as required. The desired consistency of a masala is thick and creamy.

To serve, season with the garam masala and garnish with coriander.

**Ginger**
diuretic, fat metabolism
**Cinnamon**
appetite suppressant, glucose and fat metabolism
**Turmeric**
fat metabolism
**Chilli**
fat metabolism, metabolism booster
**Coriander**
diuretic

# Peach, Fig and Crispy Serrano Ham Salad with Orange Blossom and Ginger Dressing 320 kcal/10.5g fat

**Serves 2**

You might be surprised to learn that peaches are part of the rose family and originate from China, where their kernels are used to treat inflammation. Predictably, what traditional Chinese medicine has known for aeons is now in peachy kilter with today's scientific understanding of fruit and its anti-inflammatory and weight-loss effect on the body. This is a feast for the eyes as well as the stomach: it is the beautiful salad which adorns the cover of this book.

**For the dressing**
**1 tablespoon olive oil**
**1 teaspoon mustard seeds**
**1 tablespoon balsamic vinegar**
**1 teaspoon grated fresh root
  ginger**
**1 tablespoon orange blossom
  honey**

**For the salad**
**50g Serrano ham**
**3 large ripe peaches, sliced**
**100g ripe figs, quartered**
**1 small red onion, thinly sliced**
**60g rocket leaves**
**20g baby spinach leaves**
**a handful of fresh basil leaves**
**freshly ground black pepper, to
  taste**

To make the dressing, pour the olive oil into a deep saucepan, add the mustard seeds and cook on a high heat until the seeds start to pop. Set aside and allow to cool.

In a small bowl combine the balsamic vinegar with the ginger. Now slowly pour in the honey, stirring. Finally mix in the mustard seed oil. This is your dressing.

Grill the slices of Serrano ham until crisp and set aside. Put the peach slices and fig quarters in a salad bowl with the onion, rocket, spinach and basil. Pour over the salad dressing and toss well. Plate up the salad and serve with shards of Serrano ham and plenty of black pepper.

**Mustard**
fat metabolism
**Ginger**
diuretic, fat metabolism
**Black pepper**
fat metabolism, metabolism booster

# Black-eyed Wraps

355 kcal/7.5g fat

**Serves 4**

Beans are rich in soluble fibre, which is not easily broken down by your body. Many of these black-eyed beans will pass straight through your digestive system. Great news for keeping a tab on your weight.

**½ tablespoon olive oil**
**1 teaspoon cumin seeds**
**1 garlic clove, sliced**
**1 small red onion, sliced**
**50ml passata**
**½ teaspoon sugar**
**400g can black-eyed beans,**
  **rinsed and drained**
**120g cherry tomatoes**
**1 teaspoon smoked paprika**
**2 spring onions, thinly sliced**
**1 tablespoon chopped fresh**
  **coriander**
**sea salt, to taste**
**4 wholemeal wraps**

Put the olive oil and cumin seeds in a non-stick saucepan and cook over a medium-high heat until the seeds start to sizzle – this should take no longer than 1-2 minutes. Remove the pan from the heat and allow it to cool for a moment. Now add the sliced garlic to the pan and heat on a medium-low temperature until the garlic sizzles. Add the onion and cook for about 5 minutes or until the onion softens slightly, stirring frequently.

Add the passata, sugar, beans, cherry tomatoes and paprika. Cook, semi-covered, over a low heat for 15 minutes, stirring from time to time. Mix in the spring onions and coriander and season with salt to taste. Allow to cool for a few moments.

Divide the bean mixture equally between the wholemeal wraps, placing the beans in the centre of the wrap. Fold up and slice in half before serving.

**Coriander**
diuretic

# Half-pounder Beef Burgers on Toasted Sesame Bagels

## 360 kcal/10g fat

**Serves 4**

Try getting your mitts on grass-fed beef steak mince which contains long-chain omega-3 fatty acids, similar to those found in oily fish. According to scientists from the University of Navarra, 'a diet rich in long-chain omega-3 fatty acids modulated satiety in overweight and obese volunteers during weight loss'. Patting a cow in a paddock does not count.

**For the burgers**
**500g extra lean beef steak mince**
**1 egg**
**1 medium onion, finely chopped**
**2 tablespoons chopped flat-leaf parsley**
**1 tablespoon grated fresh root ginger**
**2 cloves garlic, finely chopped**
**1 red chilli (optional), deseeded and chopped**
**1 tablespoon soy sauce**
**1 teaspoon sugar**
**2 teaspoons cumin seeds**
**1 teaspoon smoked paprika**
**½ teaspoon freshly ground black pepper**

**For everything else**
**2 tablespoons low-fat Greek yogurt**
**2 teaspoons full-fat mayonnaise**
**1 tablespoon chopped fresh dill**
**2 sesame bagels, cut in half**
**1 tomato, sliced**
**¼ cucumber, sliced**
**4 slices pickled cucumber (optional)**
**wholegrain mustard**
**1 small red onion, sliced**
**50g rocket leaves**

First make the burgers. Preheat the oven to 240°C/fan 220°C/Gas Mark 9 and line a baking tray with greaseproof paper. Place all the burger ingredients in a food processor and blitz until the meat is very finely chopped and all is thoroughly combined.

Shape 4 burgers and place them on the baking tray. Cook in the centre of the oven for 20 minutes, turning halfway through the cooking time.

In a small bowl, mix the yogurt with the mayonnaise and dill. Toast the bagel halves. Place each of the toasted bagel halves on a plate and spread with the yogurt sauce. Place slices of tomato on each bagel and top with a cooked burger. Arrange the slices of cucumber and pickled cucumber on top of the burger. Add a dollop of the wholegrain mustard and sprinkle over the sliced red onion and rocket leaves.

**Parsley**
diuretic, fat metabolism
**Ginger**
diuretic, fat metabolism
**Chilli**
fat metabolism, metabolism booster
**Black pepper**
fat metabolism, metabolism booster
**Dill**
diuretic, fat metabolism, metabolism booster
**Mustard**
fat metabolism

**Superfood Diet Half-pounder Beef Burger on Toasted Sesame Bagel**
360 kcal/10g fat/2400 ORAC units

**Comparable beef burger**
659 kcal/29.3g fat/ORAC units neg

# Smokin' Super-bean, Egg and Tuna Salad

## 440 kcal/16g fat

**Serves 4**

Packed with fibre and protein-rich foods, this lunchbox meal will fill you up without filling you out. Be more generous with the herbs, if you like, to lift the taste further.

**400g can flageolet beans, rinsed and drained**
**400g can black-eyed beans, rinsed and drained**
**400g can red kidney beans, rinsed and drained**
**200g can tuna in brine, drained**
**200g can sweetcorn, drained**
**1 medium red onion, diced**
**1 tomato, diced**
**1 tablespoon lemon juice**
**2 tablespoons olive oil**
**2 tablespoons chopped fresh mint**
**2 tablespoons chopped fresh basil**
**1 clove garlic, crushed**
**1 green chilli (optional), deseeded and finely sliced**
**1 teaspoon smoked paprika**
**1 teaspoon sugar**
**freshly ground black pepper and sea salt, to taste**
**4 hard-boiled eggs, quartered**
**2 spring onions, thinly sliced**

Combine all the ingredients, except the eggs and spring onions, in a large mixing bowl. Refrigerate for at least 30 minutes.

To serve, top with the hardboiled eggs and spring onions.

**Black pepper**
fat metabolism, metabolism booster

# Dinner

# At a glance...

# Red Cabbage Borscht

## 55 kcal/0.5g fat

**Serves 9**

55 calories for a soup is ace, and it certainly beats a cup-a-soup in the nutritional and filling stakes. You might be surprised to know that cooked red cabbage contains more antioxidants than raw cabbage.

**400g red cabbage, quartered and sliced**
**400g swede, peeled and chopped into large chunks**
**200g carrots, sliced**
**1 onion, sliced**
**2 cloves garlic, sliced**
**400g can chopped tomatoes**
**1 tablespoon tomato purée**
**1 tablespoon soy sauce**
**2 chicken or vegetable stock cubes, crumbled**
**1 tablespoon dried oregano**
**freshly ground black pepper and sea salt, to taste**
**chopped fresh dill, to garnish**

Place all the ingredients except the seasoning and dill in a large saucepan and cover with 1.5 litres water. Mix well, and bring to the boil. Reduce to a simmer and cover. Cook for 50 minutes, stirring occasionally.

Remove from the heat and blitz until smooth, adding extra water if necessary. Reheat the soup to serve, season to taste with black pepper and salt, and garnish with a little dill.

**Oregano**
appetite suppressant, fat metabolism
**Black pepper**
fat metabolism, metabolism booster
**Dill**
diuretic, fat metabolism, metabolism booster

# Cream of Pumpkin and Pear Soup

## 80 kcal/1g fat

**Serves 5**

Researchers from East China Normal University suggest that compounds found in pumpkin boost levels of insulin in the blood, and therefore 'pumpkin extract is potentially a very good product for pre-diabetic people, as well as for those who already have diabetes'. I think Jack-o'-Lantern is trying to tell us something.

**450g pumpkin or butternut squash, peeled and diced**
**2 large pears, peeled, cored and diced**
**1 medium onion, finely chopped**
**1 chicken or vegetable stock cube**
**1 teaspoon cumin seeds**
**freshly ground black pepper and sea salt, to taste**
**chopped fresh coriander, to garnish**

Place the diced pumpkin or butternut squash, diced pears, chopped onion and stock cube in a large saucepan. Cover with 1 litre boiling water, and bring to a simmer. Cook, uncovered, for 30 minutes or until the pumpkin is soft, stirring occasionally. Blitz the soup until smooth.

Place the cumin seeds in a non-stick frying pan and heat on a medium heat until the seeds start to sizzle and pop – this should take no longer than 2 minutes. Mix the cumin seeds through the soup and reheat to serve. Season to taste with black pepper and salt, and garnish with coriander.

**Black pepper**
fat metabolism, metabolism booster
**Coriander**
diuretic

**The Superfood Diet**

Left: Cream of Pumpkin and Pear Soup, page 111
This page: Slim Noodles with Samphire, Mint and Chilli, page 114

# Slim Noodles with Samphire, Mint and Chilli

## 80 kcal/7.5g fat

**Serves 2**

By swapping egg noodles for Slim Noodles, you can rocket-launch more than a whopping 300 calories into the ethersphere and well away from your hips.

**1 tablespoon walnut oil**
**4 cloves garlic, sliced**
**100g samphire, washed thoroughly and patted dry on kitchen paper**
**1 green chilli, deseeded and sliced**
**400g Slim Noodles, rinsed and drained**
**2 handfuls of fresh mint leaves**
**freshly ground black pepper, to taste**
**lemon wedges, to serve**

Pour the walnut oil into a deep non-stick saucepan, add the garlic and cook on a medium heat until the garlic starts to sizzle – this should take no longer than 1 minute. Add the samphire and continue to cook, stirring frequently, for 1 minute or until the samphire turns a bright green colour.

Mix through the sliced chilli until heated through. Now add the drained noodles and mint leaves and continue stirring until heated through. Season with black pepper and serve with the lemon wedges.

**Chilli**
fat metabolism, metabolism booster
**Black pepper**
fat metabolism, metabolism booster

# Poached Chicken and Vegetable Broth

## 100 kcal/2g fat

**Serves 4**

Spices such as cinnamon, ginger and chilli interact with fat at a cellular level, helping to break it down and thus boosting your weight-loss efforts.

1 large carrot, peeled and diced into 1cm cubes
1 medium potato, peeled and diced into 1cm cubes
1 stalk of lemongrass, finely chopped
1 stick of cinnamon
1 star anise
4 green cardamom pods, lightly crushed
1 chicken stock cube, crumbled
200g skinless chicken breast
1 teaspoon grated fresh root ginger
1 teaspoon tamarind paste
1 tablespoon fish sauce
2 tablespoons lime juice
a handful of petits pois (fresh or frozen)
1 spring onion, finely sliced
1 tablespoon chopped fresh coriander
finely sliced deseeded red chilli, to taste

Place the carrot, potato, lemongrass, cinnamon stick, star anise, cardamoms and chicken stock cube in a medium saucepan. Add 1 litre water and bring to the boil. Reduce to a simmer and cook, uncovered, for 10 minutes.

After 10 minutes, add the whole chicken breast to the pan (making sure the chicken is fully immersed in the broth) and bring to a simmer. Remove the pan from the heat, cover and leave the broth to stand for 3 hours to allow the chicken to poach and cook through.

Once the chicken is poached, discard the cinnamon stick, star anise and cardamoms. Remove the chicken breast and dice, and set aside.

Add the grated ginger, tamarind paste, fish sauce, lime juice and petits pois to the broth and bring to a simmer. Cook gently for 2 minutes. Add the diced chicken and heat through.

Divide the soup equally between 4 bowls and garnish with the spring onion, coriander and chilli.

**Cinnamon**
appetite suppressant, glucose and fat metabolism
**Ginger**
diuretic, fat metabolism
**Coriander**
diuretic
**Chilli**
fat metabolism, metabolism booster

# Polish Chicken and Red Cabbage Bigos

## 210 kcal/6g fat

**Serves 4**

Here is a nifty way to get friends and family eating more vegetables without any complaints.
The bioavailability of red cabbage antioxidants is increased dramatically by cooking. Indian spices work in sync with this national dish of Poland to further enhance nutrients and taste.

**1 teaspoon ground fenugreek**
**¼ teaspoon asafoetida**
**1 tablespoon cornflour**
**300g skinless chicken breasts, diced into small pieces**
**juice of 1 lemon**
**1 tablespoon olive oil**
**1 teaspoon cumin seeds**
**1 teaspoon coriander seeds**
**1 bay leaf**
**1 large onion, sliced**
**600g red cabbage, sliced**
**2 carrots, sliced**
**1 red pepper, sliced**
**2 tablespoons soy sauce**
**1 teaspoon smoked paprika**
**½ teaspoon chilli powder (optional)**
**freshly ground black pepper**

In a large bowl, mix together the fenugreek, asafoetida and cornflour. Mix through the chicken breast pieces and lemon juice and set aside.

Pour the olive oil into a deep non-stick pan and add the cumin and coriander seeds. Cook on a medium heat until the cumin seeds start to pop – this should take no longer than 2 minutes. Add the bay leaf and onion and cook until the onion starts to brown – this will take approximately 5 minutes and you will need to stir frequently.

Add the spice-coated chicken pieces and cook, stirring frequently, until the meat is browned – this should take no longer than 5 minutes.

Mix through the cabbage, carrots, red pepper, soy sauce, paprika, and chilli powder if using. Simmer, uncovered, and stirring frequently, for 20 minutes or until the cabbage is tender. Season to taste with black pepper and serve.

**Fenugreek**
fat metabolism
**Coriander**
diuretic
**Chilli**
fat metabolism, metabolism booster
**Black pepper**
fat metabolism, metabolism booster

**Dinner**

# Superfoods Toad in the Hole

## 220 kcal/5.5g fat

**Serves 8**

Spelt flour means an altogether healthier take on a hearty favourite that would otherwise be off-limits.

**8 low-fat pork sausages**
**225g white spelt flour**
**½ teaspoon turmeric**
**4 eggs**
**1 tablespoon wholegrain mustard**
**250ml semi-skimmed milk**
**freshly ground black pepper and**
    **sea salt, to taste**
**2 tablespoons chopped fresh**
    **sage leaves**

Preheat the oven to 220°C/fan 200°C/Gas Mark 7. Line a roasting tin (approximately  30 x 25 cm) with greaseproof paper and arrange the sausages in the tin.

Bake the sausages in the centre of the oven for 10 minutes. Increase the oven temperature to the maximum setting and continue baking for another 5 minutes.

In a large bowl, whisk together the flour, turmeric, eggs, mustard and half the milk until smooth. Now pour in the rest of the milk, whisking until a smooth, thin batter is achieved. Add seasoning to taste.

Remove the sausages from the oven. Ladle over the batter and sprinkle on the sage. Return the tin to the oven and reduce the temperature back to 220°C/fan 200°C/Gas Mark 7. Bake for 30-35 minutes, or until the mixture is risen and brown.

**Turmeric**
fat metabolism
**Mustard**
fat metabolism
**Black pepper**
fat metabolism, metabolism booster
**Sage**
diuretic

**Superfood Diet Toad in the Hole**
220 kcal/5.5g fat/400 ORAC units

**Comparable toad in the hole**
993 kcal/77.1g fat/ORAC units neg

# Superfoods Chilli

225 kcal/5g fat

**Serves 6**

My lighter chilli is made with soya beans, and turkey meat which contains more protein than other meats. Soya beans are a champion superfood, and a recent study from Soochow University in China demonstrated that 'Soya protein supplementation significantly decreased body weight, fat mass and waist circumference in an overweight and obese population'. Don't let soya and its health benefits pass by, when the only thing that should be slipping away is your body fat.

**100g soya beans**
**500g lean turkey breast, diced**
**2 large onions, diced**
**2 carrots, diced**
**3 teaspoons cumin seeds**
**2 teaspoons dried oregano**
**2 teaspoons smoked paprika**
**1 teaspoon ground cinnamon**
**1 teaspoon coriander seeds**
**1 teaspoon dried chilli flakes**
**4 cloves garlic, coarsely chopped**
**400g can chopped tomatoes**

**1 tablespoon tomato purée**
**1 chicken stock cube, crumbled**
**1 tablespoon soy sauce**
**1 tablespoon chopped fresh**
**  coriander**
**Tabasco sauce and sea salt,**
**  to taste**

Place the soya beans in a large bowl and cover with plenty of cold water. Cover the bowl and leave to soak overnight.

Combine all the remaining ingredients, except the fresh coriander and Tabasco, in another large bowl. Cover and place in the refrigerator to marinate overnight.

Once the beans are soaked, rinse them in plenty of cold water and place them in a medium saucepan. Pour over boiling water and boil, uncovered, for 30 minutes. Drain and set aside.

Remove the bowl of marinating meat and vegetables from the refrigerator and turn into a large saucepan. Add 750ml boiling water and the drained soya beans. Set over a medium heat and bring to a gentle simmer, stirring well. Cook, uncovered, for 1 hour, stirring from time to time.

Remove the pan from the heat, stir in the freshly chopped coriander, and season to taste with Tabasco and salt.

**Oregano**
appetite suppressant, fat metabolism
**Cinnamon**
appetite suppressant, glucose and fat metabolism
**Coriander**
diuretic
**Chilli**
fat metabolism, metabolism booster

**Superfood Diet Chilli**
225 kcal/5g fat

**Comparable chilli con carne**
776 kcal/24.8g fat

# Chicken Katsu Curry

230 kcal/7.5g fat

**Serves 4**

Say no to traditional chicken 'fatsu' and keep your inner sumo, well, inner.

**1 tablespoon sesame oil**
**1 medium onion, diced**
**1 green pepper, diced**
**2 cloves garlic, sliced**
**1 tablespoon grated fresh root ginger**
**1 tablespoon curry powder**
**½ teaspoon ground fenugreek**
**½ teaspoon chilli flakes**
**500g skinless chicken breasts, diced into small pieces**
**2 tablespoons cornflour**
**1 tablespoon soy sauce**
**1 teaspoon light brown soft sugar**
**1 chicken stock cube, crumbled**

Pour the sesame oil into a deep non-stick pan and add the onion, green pepper, garlic and ginger. Cook on a medium heat, stirring frequently, for about 5 minutes or until the onion has softened slightly.

Remove the pan from the heat and stir in the curry powder, fenugreek and chilli flakes. Return the pan to a low-medium heat and continue cooking for 1 minute, stirring frequently. Add the diced chicken and cook for about 5 minutes, stirring frequently, until the chicken is sealed all over. Mix in the cornflour and continue to cook until heated through.

Slowly pour in 500ml cold water, stirring all the time. Bring to a simmer and add the soy sauce, sugar and crumbled stock cube. Simmer gently, uncovered, for 10 minutes, stirring frequently. Serve immediately.

**Ginger**
diuretic, fat metabolism
**Turmeric (in curry powder)**
fat metabolism
**Fenugreek**
fat metabolism
**Chilli**
fat metabolism, metabolism booster

**Superfood Diet Chicken Katsu Curry**
230 kcal/7.5g fat

**Comparable chicken katsu curry**
1103 kcal/44.9g fat

# Thai Green Curry with Poached Seafood

235 kcal/11.5g fat

**Serves 4**

A rich Thai curry back on the menu, yet one you can enjoy without feeling guilty.

**1 stalk of lemongrass, cut into small pieces and soaked in a little boiling water**
**1 tablespoon green curry paste**
**200ml light coconut milk**
**200g low-fat Greek yogurt**
**1 tablespoon grated fresh root ginger**
**2 cloves garlic, sliced**
**1 teaspoon grated lime rind**
**1 tablespoon fish sauce**
**1 teaspoon sugar**
**4 kaffir lime leaves, sliced**
**a small handful of fresh Thai basil, chopped**
**100g aubergine, diced**
**300g fish pie mix**
**a small handful of mangetout**
**a small handful of petits pois (fresh or frozen)**
**10g chopped fresh coriander**
**10g chopped fresh dill**

Place the lemongrass pieces, curry paste, coconut milk, yogurt, ginger, garlic, lime rind, fish sauce and sugar in a food processor. Blitz until smooth.

Pour the blended curry mixture into a deep saucepan. Add the kaffir lime leaves, basil and aubergine and bring to a simmer on a medium heat. Simmer gently for 10 minutes, uncovered.

Now add the fish pie mix, mangetout and petits pois. Return to a simmer, then remove from the heat, cover and leave to stand for 5 minutes, to allow the fish to poach and cook through.

Mix through the coriander and dill and serve.

**Chilli (in curry paste)**
fat metabolism, metabolism booster
**Ginger**
diuretic, fat metabolism
**Coriander**
diuretic
**Dill**
diuretic, fat metabolism, metabolism booster

**Superfood Diet Thai Green Curry with Poached Seafood**
235 kcal/11.5g fat

**Comparable Thai green curry**
711 kcal/46g fat

Above: Chicken Katsu Curry, page 122
Right: Superfoods Sweet Potato and Pumpkin Fish Pie, page 128

　　　　　　　　**The Superfood Diet**

# Superfoods Cottage Pie

245 kcal/6g fat

**Serves 6**

Bartering half the potato for pumpkin or butternut squash is a neat food swap as each of these gourds contains approximately one quarter of the calories of our dearly beloved 'couch' potato.

**1 tablespoon olive oil**
**1 leek, sliced**
**3 carrots, peeled and grated**
**2 cloves garlic, sliced**
**500g lean turkey breast mince**
**2 tablespoons chopped fresh
    sage leaves**
**2 tablespoons tomato purée**
**Worcestershire sauce, to taste**
**500ml beef stock**
**500g potato, peeled and cut into
    large bite-sized pieces**
**500g pumpkin or butternut
    squash, peeled and cut into
    large bite-sized pieces**
**½ teaspoon cumin seeds**
**1 teaspoon turmeric**
**½ teaspoon chilli powder (optional)**
**freshly ground black pepper and
    sea salt, to taste**
**1 tablespoon fresh rosemary
    leaves**

**Superfood Diet Cottage Pie**
245 kcal/6g fat/4260 ORAC units

**Comparable Cottage Pie**
660 kcal/34g fat/2280 ORAC units

Pour ½ tablespoon olive oil into a non-stick pan. Add the leek, carrots and garlic and cook on a medium heat, stirring regularly, until the leeks are soft - this should take no longer than 7 minutes. Add the turkey mince and sage leaves and cook on a medium-high temperature, stirring constantly, until the meat s sealed all over – this should take no more than about 5 minutes. Add the tomato purée and a splash of Worcestershire sauce, mixing well to incorporate. Pour in the beef stock and simmer gently, uncovered, for 20 minutes, stirring from time to time. Cover and keep warm.

Meanwhile make the mash for the topping. Fill a deep saucepan with water and bring to the boil. Add the potato and pumpkin or butternut squash pieces to the pan, return to the boil, cover and cook for about 15 minutes or until the vegetables are just tender. Drain well and set aside.

Pour another ½ tablespoon olive oil into a separate large saucepan, add the cumin seeds and cook over a low-medium heat until the seeds begin to pop – this will take no longer than about 2 minutes. Remove the pan from the heat and add the turmeric, stirring all the time. Add the chilli powder, if using, pepper and salt. Return the pan to the heat  and cook for a further 20 seconds, mixing well.

Remove the pan from the heat. Add the cooked vegetables to the spice mixture and mash well. Mix through the rosemary leaves and then cover, set aside and keep warm. Preheat the oven to 220°C/fan 200°C/Gas Mark 7.

Place the cooked turkey mince mixture in a 23cm square ovenproof dish. Spread the mashed potato mixture evenly over the top. Using a fork, scrape the top of the mash to create a ruffled surface. Bake in the centre of the oven for 40 minutes or until the top starts to colour and the mince is bubbling up over the top of the mash.

**Turmeric**
fat metabolism
**Chilli**
fat metabolism, metabolism booster
**Black pepper**
fat metabolism, metabolism booster
**Rosemary**
diuretic, fat metabolism

# Superspices Spaghetti Bolognaise

245 kcal/8.5g fat

**Serves 4**

With help from Slim Pasta spaghetti, you will eliminate approximately 300 calories from a traditional spaghetti bolognaise meal. A life-changing epiphany for big eaters like me.

**1 tablespoon olive oil**
**10 green cardamom pods, lightly crushed**
**1 small onion, thinly sliced**
**4 cloves garlic, sliced**
**250g lean turkey thigh mince**
**1 litre passata**
**1 tablespoon grated fresh root ginger**
**1–2 green chillies (optional), chopped**
**2 teaspoons dried oregano**
**2 bay leaves**
**a large handful of fresh basil leaves, coarsely chopped**
**1 carrot, grated**
**800g Slim Pasta spaghetti, prepared according to packet instructions, rinsed in cold water and drained**
**freshly ground black pepper and sea salt, to taste**

Pour the olive oil into a deep non-stick pan, add the cardamom pods and cook over a low-medium heat until they start to pop – this should take no longer than 2–3 minutes. Add the onion and fry until the onion is light brown in colour, remembering to stir frequently – this should take no more than 5 minutes. Stir in the garlic and fry for about 2 minutes or until the garlic is a light brown colour.

Mix in the turkey mince and cook, stirring, until it is sealed all over – this should take no more than about 5 minutes. Add 250ml of the passata, together with the ginger, chillies if using, oregano, bay leaves and basil. Cook for about 5 minutes, stirring occasionally, until the excess juices in the pan have dried off. Add the grated carrot and remaining passata, mix and bring to a gentle simmer.

Simmer gently, covered, for 20 minutes, stirring from time to time. After 20 minutes, uncover and continue to cook gently for a further 20 minutes, stirring from time to time.

Remove the cardamom pods and bay leaves, mix through the Slim Pasta spaghetti and heat through. Season to taste with pepper and salt.

**Ginger**
diuretic, fat metabolism
**Chilli**
fat metabolism, metabolism booster
**Oregano**
appetite suppressant, fat metabolism

**Superfood Diet Superspices Spaghetti Bolognaise**
245 kcal/8.5g fat/3830 ORAC units

**Comparable spaghetti bolognaise**
556 kcal/27.5g fat/3300 ORAC units

# Superfoods Sweet Potato and Pumpkin Fish Pie

.245 kcal/8g fat

**Serves 6**

Turmeric aids cell metabolism and, in particular, fat metabolism – as attested by research from the University of Texas. Perhaps a 21st century Mary Poppins would sing about turmeric rather than sugar?

**650g fish pie mix**
**1 teaspoon smoked paprika**
**2 tablespoons chopped fresh dill**
**freshly ground black pepper, to taste**
**500g sweet potatoes, peeled and cut into large bite-sized pieces**
**500g pumpkin or butternut squash, peeled and cut into large bite-sized pieces**
**½ tablespoon olive oil**
**1 teaspoon cumin seeds**
**½ teaspoon mustard seeds**
**1 teaspoon turmeric**
**½ teaspoon chilli powder**
**a large handful of green peas (fresh or frozen)**
**1 carrot, grated**
**1 stick of celery, grated**
**50g baby spinach leaves**
**lemon wedges, to serve**

In a large bowl, combine the fish pie mix, paprika, dill and pepper. Cover and reserve in the refrigerator.

Make the mash for the pie topping. Fill a deep saucepan with water and bring to the boil. Add the sweet potato and pumpkin pieces to the pan, return to the boil, cover and cook for about 15 minutes or until the vegetables are just tender. Drain well and set aside.

Pour the olive oil into a separate deep non-stick pan, add the cumin and mustard seeds and cook over a medium heat until the seeds begin to pop – this will take no longer than 2–3 minutes. Remove the pan from the heat and mix through the turmeric, stirring all the time. Add the chilli powder, return to the heat and cook for a further 20 seconds, stirring well.

Remove the pan from the heat again. Add the cooked vegetables to the spice mixture and mash well. Mix through the green peas, then cover, set aside and keep warm.

Preheat the oven to 220°C/fan 200°C/Gas Mark 7. Add the carrot, celery and baby spinach leaves to the reserved spicy fish pie mix and combine thoroughly. Turn the mixture into a square 23cm square ovenproof dish. Spread the mash evenly over the top of the fish and vegetable mixture. Using a fork, scrape the top of the mash to create a ruffled surface.

Bake the pie in the centre of the oven for 40 minutes. Serve with the lemon wedges.

**Dill**
diuretic, fat metabolism, metabolism booster
**Black pepper**
fat metabolism, metabolism booster
**Mustard**
fat metabolism
**Turmeric**
fat metabolism
**Chilli**
fat metabolism, metabolism booster

**Superfood Diet Sweet Potato and Pumpkin Fish Pie**
245 kcal/8g fat/2830 ORAC units

**Comparable Fish Pie**
557 kcal/22g fat/1960 ORAC units

# Pasta Carbonara

245 kcal/12.5g fat

**Serves 2**

If you thought you'd have to give up on a favourite: think again!

**2 teaspoons cornflour**
**1 teaspoon dried oregano**
**200g low-fat Greek yogurt**
**½ tablespoon olive oil**
**1 small onion, diced**
**2 cloves garlic, sliced**
**100g smoked ham, diced**
**120g mushrooms, sliced**
**800g Slim Pasta spaghetti or**
**    fettuccine, prepared according**
**    to packet instructions, rinsed in**
**    cold water and drained**
**1 egg, whisked**
**freshly ground black pepper, to**
**    taste**

In a small bowl thoroughly combine the cornflour, oregano and yogurt. Set aside.

Pour the olive oil into a non-stick frying pan and add the onion and garlic. Fry on a medium heat, stirring frequently, until the onion is soft and the garlic is golden brown in colour – this should take no longer then 5 minutes. Add the ham and mushrooms and continue to cook until the mushrooms have softened.

Now add the drained Slim Pasta and heat thoroughly, stirring frequently. Pour the yogurt mixture slowly into the frying pan and bring to a simmer on a low heat. Cook for 5 minutes, stirring frequently. Finally, mix in the egg, stirring rapidly. Remove from the heat. Season to taste with pepper and serve without delay.

**Oregano**
appetite suppressant, fat metabolism
**Black pepper**
fat metabolism, metabolism booster

**Superfood Diet Pasta Carbonara**
245 kcal/12.5g fat

**Comparable pasta carbonara**
2500 kcal/85g fat

# Turkey and Sushi Rice Meatballs in Passata Sauce

260 kcal/5.5g fat

**Serves 5**

Lean turkey breast mince contains considerably less fat than other breast meat. The only problem I have with it is how to get it to stick to make meatballs. This is where gooey sushi rice comes to the rescue, ingeniously redeeming what is now most certainly a sticky situation.

**500g lean turkey breast mince**
**100g Sushi Rice Pilau, chilled (see page 174)**
**1 medium onion, finely diced**
**2 tablespoons chopped fresh dill**
**1 egg**
**freshly ground black pepper and sea salt, to taste**
**½ tablespoon olive oil**
**2 cloves garlic, sliced**
**500ml passata**
**1 teaspoon sugar**
**1 teaspoon smoked paprika**
**a handful of fresh basil leaves, coarsely chopped**

In a large mixing bowl, combine the turkey mince, sushi rice pilau, onion, dill, egg, pepper and salt. Form the mixture into 15 balls and place them in a casserole dish, making sure they do not overlap one another.

Preheat the oven to 200°C/fan 180°C/Gas Mark 6. Pour the olive oil into a non-stick frying pan, add the garlic and cook on a medium heat, stirring frequently, until the garlic is browned all over – this should take no longer than 2-3 minutes. Mix in the passata, sugar, paprika and basil, with more black pepper to season, and bring to a simmer.

Pour the sauce over the meatballs in the casserole dish. Cook in the centre of the preheated oven for 45 minutes.

**Dill**
diuretic, fat metabolism, metabolism booster
**Black pepper**
fat metabolism, metabolism booster

**Superfood Diet Turkey and Sushi Rice Meatballs in Passata Sauce**
260 kcal/5.5g fat/1360 ORAC units

**Comparable meatballs**
545 kcal/36.7g fat/1045 ORAC units

# Beef and Seaweed Rendang

260 kcal/12.5g fat

**Serves 4**

Much of the fat in this rendang comes from coconut oil, which actually helps your body to burn more energy by increasing its metabolic rate. Nutty I know, but the scientists are agreed on it.

**3 shallots, halved**
**5 cloves garlic**
**3 red bird's eye chillies, sliced**
**3 tablespoons grated fresh root ginger**
**500g lean chuck steak, diced**
**400ml light coconut milk**
**2 small stalks of lemongrass, sliced lengthways**
**1 stick of cinnamon**
**1 star anise**
**6 kaffir lime leaves**
**1 tablespoon soy sauce**
**1 teaspoon sugar**
**1 teaspoon turmeric**
**2 tablespoons sea salad or 1 sheet of sushi nori, torn into small pieces (both optional)**

Blitz the shallots, garlic, chillies and ginger with 200ml water and pour this mixture into a deep saucepan. Add the diced steak, coconut milk, lemongrass, cinnamon stick, star anise, kaffir lime leaves, soy sauce, sugar and turmeric. Pour in 600ml boiling water.

Bring to a gentle simmer and cook, uncovered, stirring from time to time, for 2 hours or until the meat is tender. If the sauce dries out too much, add a very little water as required. At the end of cooking, the sauce should resemble a thick masala.

Remove the lemongrass, cinnamon stick, star anise and kaffir lime leaves. Garnish with the sea salad or sushi nori, if using, and serve.

**Chilli**
fat metabolism, metabolism booster
**Ginger**
diuretic, fat metabolism
**Cinnamon**
appetite suppressant, glucose and fat metabolism
**Turmeric**
fat metabolism

**Superfood Diet Beef and Seaweed Rendang**
260 kcal/12.5g fat

**Comparable beef rendang**
654 kcal/54.5g fat

# Beef Stew with Gluten-free Polenta Dumplings

275 kcal/6g fat

**Serves 8**

Never could one imagine that the flavours of so many continents could be fused together so harmoniously, yet this is a dish as unmistakably British as it is Vietnamese or African. The gluten-free dumplings are made from cornmeal instead of wheat flour. Less gluten means better digestion and energy levels for your body.

**For the stew**
**1kg lean chuck steak, diced**
**2 cloves garlic, sliced**
**1 tablespoon grated fresh root ginger**
**1 green tea bag**
**2 tablespoons tomato purée**
**2 teaspoons Chinese five-spice powder**
**1 stick of cinnamon**
**3 star anise**
**1 tablespoon fish sauce**
**2 teaspoons sugar**
**2 beef stock cubes, crumbled**
**2 carrots, sliced**
**8 shallots**
**50g green peas (fresh or frozen)**

**For the dumplings**
**1 tablespoon fresh rosemary leaves, finely chopped**
**½ teaspoon red chilli flakes (optional)**
**160g cornmeal**

Place all the stew ingredients, except for the carrots, shallots and green peas, in a deep saucepan. Pour in 2 litres boiling water and bring to a gentle simmer. Cook, uncovered, stirring from time to time, for 1½ hours, removing the green tea bag after 30 minutes.

Add the carrots and shallots to the stew and continue cooking for a further 15 minutes.

In the meantime, make the dumplings. Put 500ml water in a medium saucepan with the rosemary and chilli flakes. Bring to the boil, reduce the heat to medium-low and gradually whisk in the cornmeal. Keep whisking over the heat for about 2 minutes or until the mixture is very thick. Remove from the heat and allow to cool slightly. Shape into 8 dumplings, using the palms of your hands.

Stir the green peas into the stew, then place the dumplings on top and cover the pan. Continue cooking the stew for another 15 minutes. Remove the cinnamon stick and star anise before serving.

**Ginger**
diuretic, fat metabolism
**Cinnamon**
appetite suppressant, glucose and fat metabolism
**Rosemary**
diuretic, fat metabolism
**Chilli**
fat metabolism, metabolism booster

**Beef Stew with Gluten-free Polenta Dumplings**
275 kcal/6g fat/3080 ORAC units

**Comparable beef stew with dumplings**
830 kcal/51.8g fat/430 ORAC units

Left: Beef Stew with Gluten-free Polenta Dumplings, page 133
This page: Chinese Restaurant-style Lemon Chicken, page 136

# Chinese Restaurant-style Lemon Chicken

## 285 kcal/6g fat

**Serves 4**

A Chinese restaurant favourite and an utter calorie bomb, here slapped into shape without sacrificing on taste. Coating the chicken in cornflour gives the familiar crispy-chewy Chinese texture that we all love.

**3 tablespoons cornflour**
**500g skinless chicken breasts, diced into small pieces**
**½ tablespoon sesame oil**
**2 cloves garlic, sliced**
**6 fresh root ginger batons, roughly same size as matchsticks**
**1 teaspoon finely grated lemon rind**
**juice of 2 lemons**
**6 tablespoons agave nectar**
**1 chicken stock cube, crumbled**
**lemon slices, to serve**
**2 spring onions, thinly sliced**

Put the cornflour in a bowl, add the diced chicken breast, and mix well to coat evenly. Set aside.

Pour the sesame oil into a deep non-stick pan and add the garlic and ginger. Cook on a medium heat, stirring frequently, for about 2 minutes or until the garlic is browned.

Add the chicken pieces with any excess cornflour to the pan and cook on a low heat, stirring frequently, for 5 minutes or until the chicken is browned all over. Be careful not to burn the cornflour.

Slowly pour in 400ml cold water, stirring all the time. Bring to a simmer on a medium heat and add the lemon rind and juice, agave nectar and stock cube. Simmer gently, uncovered, for 10 minutes. Garnish with lemon slices and spring onions and serve immediately.

**Ginger**
diuretic, fat metabolism

**Superfood Diet Chinese Restaurant-style Lemon Chicken**
285 kcal/6g fat/975 ORAC units

**Comparable restaurant-style lemon chicken**
1340 kcal/74g fat/275 ORAC units

**The Superfood Diet**

# Chicken and Passion Fruit Shish Kebabs

320 kcal/6.5g fat

**Serves 4**

Passion fruit has a miraculous effect on chicken, making it tender beyond belief while adding its own uplifting flavour and crunch. Passion fruit enzymes have a positive effect on your body, too, by helping to break down food – therefore aiding digestion and weight loss.

**For the kebabs**
**450g skinless chicken breasts, cut into 4cm cubes**
**3 passion fruits, halved, pulp and seeds scooped out**
**4 cloves garlic, sliced**
**1 tablespoon grated fresh root ginger**
**2 green chillies (optional), deseeded and finely chopped**
**4 tablespoons low-fat Greek yogurt**
**1 teaspoon ground coriander**
**sea salt, to taste**
**1 tablespoon olive oil**
**20g bunch of fresh coriander, chopped**
**2 green peppers, cut into 4cm pieces**

**For the kachumber**
**2 tomatoes, diced**
**1 red onion, diced**
**1 tablespoon chopped fresh mint**
**1 tablespoon chopped fresh parsley**
**1 tablespoon lemon juice**

**For the raita**
**125g low-fat Greek yogurt**
**1 teaspoon full-fat mayonnaise**
**1 teaspoon smoked paprika**

**For serving**
**4 wholemeal pitta breads**

First prepare the chicken for the kebabs. Place the chicken cubes in a bowl and set aside. Put the passion fruit pulp and seeds, garlic, ginger, chillies if using, yogurt, ground coriander, salt, olive oil and fresh coriander in a food processor and blitz until smooth. Pour the mixture over the chicken cubes, and mix well. Cover and place in the refrigerator to marinate for a minimum of 12 hours, maximum 24 hours.

To make the kachumber, mix the tomatoes, onion, mint and parsley with the lemon juice in a small bowl and set aside.

For the raita, combine the yogurt, mayonnaise and paprika in another small bowl and set aside.

To complete the kebabs, remove the chicken from the refrigerator. Soak 4 skewers in cold water for at least 20 minutes. Preheat the grill to high. Assemble the skewers by alternating cubes of chicken with pieces of green pepper. Grill the kebabs for 15 minutes, turning halfway through cooking. Set aside.

Put the pittas under the grill until warmed through. Divide the kebabs, kachumber, raita and warm pittas between 4 plates and serve immediately.

**Ginger**
diuretic, fat metabolism
**Chilli**
fat metabolism, metabolism booster
**Coriander**
diuretic
**Parsley**
diuretic, fat metabolism

**Superfood Diet Chicken and Passion Fruit Shish Kebab**
320 kcal/6.5g fat/2560 ORAC units

**Comparable chicken shish kebab**
415 kcal/8g fat/1005 ORAC units

The Superfood Diet

Left: Chicken and Passion Fruit Shish Kebabs, page 137
This page: Superfoods Chicken and Mushroom Pie, page 142

# Superfoods Italian Lentil and Brown Rice Stew

## 325 kcal/3g fat

**Serves 5**

Not all calories are the same. It has to be good news for slimmers that one third of the calories in high-fibre brown lentils remain undigested.

**260g brown lentils**
**170g Italian brown rice**
**2 medium onions, diced**
**400g can chopped tomatoes**
**1 chicken or vegetable stock
    cube, crumbled**
**1 tablespoon soy sauce**
**1 teaspoon dried oregano**
**1 carrot, grated**
**a large handful of petits pois
    (fresh or frozen)**

Place the lentils, rice, onions, tomatoes, stock cube, soy sauce, oregano and carrot in a deep saucepan. Pour in 1.5 litres boiling water. Place over a high heat and return to the boil, then reduce the heat to low. Simmer, uncovered, for 50 minutes. Stir occasionally to avoid sticking. If the mixture thickens too much, you may need to add a little more boiling water.

Stir in the petits pois, simmer for 2-3 minutes, then serve.

**Oregano**
appetite suppressant, fat metabolism

# Chicken with Blueberries and Cinnamon

340 kcal/17g fat

**Serves 4**

My signature dish made international headlines when it appeared in my first book, *Indian Superfood*, at the start of my food-writing career. When served with Superfoods Goji Berry and Green Pea Pilau (see page 177), it contains as many antioxidants as 23 bunches of grapes – thanks to the generous use of cinnamon, blueberries and goji berries. This must be the world's healthiest meal.

**200g blueberries**
**20g fresh coriander, coarsely chopped**
**2 tablespoons grated fresh root ginger**
**sea salt, to taste**
**500g low-fat Greek yogurt**
**3 tablespoons olive oil**
**4 cloves garlic, sliced**
**1 teaspoon turmeric**
**2 tablespoons ground cinnamon**
**1 teaspoon chilli powder**
**500g skinless chicken breasts, cut into small pieces**
**1 teaspoon garam masala**
**extra chopped fresh coriander, to garnish**

In a food processor, blend together the blueberries, coriander, ginger, salt and yogurt to make a purée. Set aside.

Pour the olive oil into a deep non-stick pan. Add the garlic and cook over a low-medium heat until the garlic starts to turn a brown colour – this should take no longer than 2 minutes. Add the turmeric, mix well and and cook for about 20 seconds. Stir in the cinnamon and chilli powder and cook for a further 20 seconds. Now add the chicken pieces and cook, stirring frequently, until sealed all over – this should take no more than 5 minutes.

Slowly pour in the yogurt purée, mixing it into the chicken, then bring to a simmer over a low heat. Simmer, uncovered, for 15 minutes, stirring from time to time. Mix in the garam masala and garnish with a little more coriander.

**Coriander**
diuretic
**Ginger**
diuretic, fat metabolism
**Turmeric**
fat metabolism
**Cinnamon**
appetite suppressant, glucose and fat metabolism
**Chilli**
fat metabolism, metabolism booster

# Superfoods Chicken and Mushroom Pie

345kcal/10g fat

**Serves 4**

Hand on my heart, this light and fresh-tasting pie comes with a clean bill of health.

**For the crust**
**125g wholegrain spelt flour**
**75g white spelt flour, plus extra**
**for dusting**
**1 teaspoon dill seeds**
**¼ teaspoon fine sea salt**
**1 tablespoon olive oil**
**1 egg yolk**

**For the pie filling**
**1 tablespoon olive oil**
**6 green cardamom pods**
**(optional), lightly crushed**
**2 leeks, sliced**
**4 cloves garlic, sliced**
**1 teaspoon grated fresh root**
**ginger**
**500g skinless chicken breasts,**
**cut into small pieces**
**120g shiitake mushrooms,**
**quartered**
**500ml Cream of Oyster Mushroom**
**Soup (see page 68)**
**200g can sweetcorn, drained**
**½ chicken stock cube, crumbled**
**freshly ground black pepper,**
**to taste**
**20g fresh dill, finely chopped**

To make the crust, place the flours in a large mixing bowl and combine with the dill seeds and salt. Make a well in the centre of the flour. Slowly pour in the olive oil and 100ml cold water, while stirring with a wooden spoon and gradually mixing in the flour. When the flour is all incorporated, knead the dough for 5 minutes in the bowl (or on a lightly floured work surface) until it is firm yet elastic – the dough needs to be of a pliable texture, therefore you may need to add a few drops more of cold water to get the right consistency. Cover with a clean kitchen towel and leave to rest.

To make the pie filling, pour the olive oil and into a large non-stick pan, add the cardamom pods and heat on a medium heat until the pods start to sizzle – this should take no longer than 2-3 minutes. Add the leeks, garlic and ginger and cook, stirring frequently, until the leeks are soft – this should take no longer than 5 minutes. Now add the chicken pieces and continue cooking, stirring frequently, until the chicken is sealed – again, this should take no longer

than 5 minutes. Next, add the mushrooms and cook for about another 2 minutes, until they have softened. Finally, add the mushroom soup, sweetcorn, stock cube and pepper, and bring to a simmer. Cook gently, uncovered, for 10 minutes, stirring occasionally.

In the meantime, take the dough and place it on a lightly floured surface. Using a rolling pin, roll it out into a sheet slightly bigger than the circumference of your pie dish and no thicker than a £1 coin.

Preheat the oven to 200°C/fan 180°C/Gas Mark 6. Remove the chicken filling mixture from the heat and mix in the dill. Transfer the mixture to your pie dish. Brush the top edge of the pie dish with a little egg yolk. Place the pastry over the pie dish, pushing down the pastry against the top edge of the pie dish to seal. Cut off any excess pastry. Brush the pastry with egg yolk and, using a sharp knife, make 3 cuts in the top of the pie. Bake on the bottom oven rack for 35 minutes, or until the pastry is golden brown.

**Dill**
diuretic, fat metabolism, metabolism booster
**Ginger**
diuretic, fat metabolism
**Black pepper**
fat metabolism, metabolism booster

**Superfood Diet Chicken and Mushroom Pie**
345kcal/10g fat/3020 ORAC units

**Comparable pie**
762 kcal/49g fat/1250 ORAC units

# Mango Chicken Curry

375 kcal/7.5g fat

**Serves 4**

My best friend says this is the best thing he has ever eaten. I shall let you be the judge. But I do know that mango is a champion fruit, well documented for the part it plays in obstructing the development of fat cells.

**1 tablespoon olive oil**
**2 teaspoons fennel seeds**
**1 teaspoon nigella seeds**
**1 teaspoon mustard seeds**
**1 teaspoon fenugreek seeds**
**2 cloves garlic, sliced**
**3 tablespoons grated fresh root**
   **ginger**
**1 teaspoon turmeric**
**2 green chillies, deseeded and**
   **chopped**
**sea salt, to taste**
**½ teaspoon asafoetida**
**1 tablespoon tomato purée**
**800ml mango pulp**
**500g skinless chicken breasts,**
   **diced into small pieces**
**chopped fresh coriander, to**
   **garnish**

Pour the olive oil into a deep non-stick pan, add the fennel, nigella, mustard and fenugreek seeds and cook over a high heat until the mustard seeds start to pop – this should take no more than 1–2 minutes. Remove the pan from the heat and allow the oil to cool for a moment.

Add the garlic and ginger to the pan and cook over a low-medium heat, stirring frequently, until they are a golden brown colour – this should take no more than 3 minutes. Remove from the heat and add the turmeric, mix well and allow to stand for about 20 seconds.

Return the pan to the heat and add the chillies, salt, asafoetida, tomato purée and mango pulp. Mix well and bring to simmering point. Stir in the chicken pieces and return to a gentle simmer, then cook, uncovered, for 40 minutes, stirring from time to time. Garnish with the chopped coriander to serve.

**Mustard**
fat metabolism
**Ginger**
diuretic, fat metabolism
**Turmeric**
fat metabolism
**Chilli**
fat metabolism, metabolism booster
**Coriander**
diuretic

**Superfood Diet Mango Chicken Curry**
375 kcal/7.5g fat

**Comparable mango chicken curry**
769 kcal/32.7g fat

This page: Mango Chicken Curry, page 143
Right: Rich and Creamy Better-than-ever Chicken Tikka Masala, page 147

# Salmon and Wild Rice Biryani with Kaffir Lime

385 kcal/17g fat

**Serves 6**

Not all fats are the same. According to scientists at the University of Navarra, 'a diet rich in long-chain omega-3 fatty acids modulates satiety'. I need no convincing.

**2 tablespoons olive oil**
**2 teaspoons cumin seeds**
**1 teaspoon black peppercorns**
**10 green cardamom pods, lightly crushed**
**1 small onion, thinly sliced**
**4 cloves garlic, sliced**
**1 tablespoon grated fresh root ginger**
**2 green chillies (optional), coarsely chopped**
**2 tablespoons mild curry powder**
**350g salmon fillets, skinned and cut into large bite-sized pieces**
**400g basmati and wild rice**
**12 kaffir lime leaves**
**sea salt, to taste**
**1 potato, diced into 1.5cm cubes**
**200g cherry tomatoes, halved**
**a small handful of chopped fresh coriander**
**lemon wedges, to serve**

Pour the olive oil into a deep non-stick pan, add the cumin seeds, peppercorns and cardamom pods and cook over a low-medium heat until the seeds start to pop – this should take no more than 2–3 minutes. Add the onion and cook until it is a light brown colour, stirring frequently – this should take no more than 5 minutes. Add the garlic, ginger and chillies, if using, and continue cooking for about 3 minutes or until the garlic is brown in colour. Add the curry powder, mix well and cook for about 20 seconds.

Add the salmon pieces and cook until they are sealed all over (but not cooked through), making sure to stir gently to avoid breaking the salmon into small pieces – this should take about 2–3 minutes. Take the pan off the heat, then remove the salmon pieces to a warm plate, brushing off back into the pan any excess spice mixture that may have stuck to them. Set the salmon aside.

Return the pan to the heat and add the basmati and wild rice. Cook, stirring frequently, until the rice turns from slightly translucent to very white in colour – this process should take only about 2–3 minutes. Remove the pan from the heat.

Transfer the rice mixture into a large microwave-safe dish (at least 22 x 7cm), add the kaffir lime leaves and salt to taste and pour in 750ml boiling water. Mix well with a fork. Microwave, uncovered, for 6 minutes on HIGH at 700W, or for 5½ minutes on HIGH at 800W, or for 5 minutes on HIGH at 900W.

Mix again with a fork. Microwave, uncovered, for a further 5 minutes on HIGH at 700W, or for a further 4½ minutes on HIGH at 800W, or for a further 4 minutes on HIGH at 900W.

Mix again. Add the salmon pieces and potato cubes, making sure to cover them with the rice. Cover the dish and microwave for a further 7 minutes on HIGH at 700W, or for a further 6 minutes on HIGH at 800W, or for a further 5 minutes on HIGH at 900W.

Take the biryani out of the microwave. Stir in the cherry tomatoes, cover and leave to stand for 10 minutes. Stir in the coriander and serve with the lemon wedges.

**Black pepper**
fat metabolism, metabolism booster
**Ginger**
diuretic, fat metabolism
**Chilli (also in curry powder)**
fat metabolism, metabolism booster
**Turmeric (in curry powder)**
fat metabolism
**Coriander**
diuretic

**Superfood Diet Salmon and Wild Rice Biryani with Kaffir Lime**
385 kcal/17g fat

**Comparable restaurant biryani**
829 kcal/43.5g

# Rich and Creamy Better-than-ever Chicken Tikka Masala 400 kcal/18g fat

**Serves 4**

A dynamic 'Batman and Robin' duo come to the rescue here, with low-fat Greek yogurt and light coconut milk standing in for gut-busting dairy cream. The end result is a dish that is as creamy as the Anglo-Indian restaurant classic, yet with a smidge more of a traditional Indian slant coming from the tangy yogurt.

**2 tablespoons olive oil**
**1 teaspoon fenugreek seeds**
**15 green cardamom pods, lightly crushed**
**1 small onion, thinly sliced**
**4 cloves garlic, sliced**
**1 teaspoon ground ginger**
**2 tablespoons tandoori masala powder**
**5 tablespoons tomato purée**
**2 tablespoons grated fresh root ginger**
**2 green chillies, finely chopped**
**400g low-fat Greek yogurt**
**3 tablespoons agave nectar**
**500g skinless chicken breasts, cut into bite-sized pieces**
**400ml light coconut milk**
**sea salt, to taste**
**chopped fresh coriander, to garnish**

Pour the olive oil into a deep non-stick pan, add the fenugreek seeds and cardamom pods and cook over a low-medium heat until the oil is hot and the cardamom pods start to release their aroma – this should take no longer than 2–3 minutes. Add the onion and fry, stirring frequently, until it is light brown in colour – this should take no more than 5 minutes.

Stir in the garlic and fry for about 2 minutes or until light brown in colour. Sprinkle in the ground ginger and tandoori masala powder, mix well and cook for about 20 seconds. Add the tomato purée, fresh ginger and chillies, mix well and cook until the tomato purée is heated through – this should take no longer than 2 minutes. Pour in half of the yogurt and the agave nectar, mix well and heat through. Add the chicken pieces to the pan, mix well and cook on a medium heat, stirring all the time, until sealed all over– this should take no more than 5 minutes.

Pour in the coconut milk and the remaining yogurt and mix well. Bring to a gentle simmer, then cook, uncovered, for 40 minutes, stirring occasionally to avoid any sticking. Season to taste with salt, garnish with chopped coriander and serve.

**Fenugreek**
fat metabolism
**Ginger**
diuretic, fat metabolism
**Chilli**
fat metabolism, metabolism booster
**Coriander**
diuretic

**Superfood Diet Rich and Creamy Better-than-ever Chicken Tikka Masala**
400 kcal/18g fat

**Comparable restaurant-style chicken tikka masala**
1221 kcal/111g fat

# Heaven-is-on-Hold Salad

590 kcal/16g fat

**Serves 2**

Not for the first time, we can take advantage of the fact that not all fats are the same. The good people at the Norwegian National Institute of Nutrition advise us that omega-3 fatty acids in oily fish such as salmon can actually counteract the development of obesity. Count me in – hook, line and sinker.

**For the poached chicken**
1 stick of cinnamon
2 star anise
10 green cardamom pods, lightly
   crushed
200g skinless chicken breast

**For the salmon**
1 tablespoon tandoori masala
   powder
300g salmon fillets, skinned and
   cut into 6 large chunks
no-salt steak seasoning, to taste
1 teaspoon olive oil

**For the salad**
2 tablespoons lemon juice
1 tablespoon olive oil
sea salt, to taste
50g rocket leaves
100g cherry tomatoes, halved
1 small red onion, thinly sliced
1 tablespoon chopped fresh
   coriander
1 tablespoon chopped fresh mint
½ quantity Basmati and Wild Rice
   Pilau, warmed (see page 174)

First, poach the chicken. In a medium-sized saucepan, bring 1 litre water to the boil with the cinnamon stick, star anise and cardamoms. Simmer, covered, on a gentle heat for 10 minutes, then bring to a rapid boil. Place the chicken breast in the pan, making sure it is covered by the water, and return to the boil. Immediately take the pan off the heat and cover with a lid. Allow the chicken breast to poach in the liquid for 3 hours so that it is cooked through. (This whole procedure can be carried out in advance, even the day before, and the chicken refrigerated in the spicy brine.)

When you are ready to prepare the salad, drain the chicken and cut into chunks.

To prepare the salmon, first preheat the oven to its maximum temperature. Mix the tandoori masala powder with 2 tablespoons cold water in a small bowl. Coat the salmon chunks in this mixture. Sprinkle the steak seasoning on each side of the salmon. Pour the olive oil into a non-stick frying pan, brushing it evenly over the bottom, and heat over a medium heat. When the oil is hot, place the salmon fillets in the frying pan and cook for between 30 seconds and 1 minute on each side, or until you have a golden crust on both sides.

Transfer the seared salmon to a non-stick baking tray.

Bake the salmon at the top of the hot oven for 5 minutes. Once cooked, set aside and keep warm.

To assemble the salad, mix the lemon juice, olive oil and salt to taste in a large bowl. Add the poached chicken chunks, rocket, cherry tomatoes, onion, coriander and mint. Toss the salad to coat in the dressing.

Divide the warm salmon chunks between 2 dinner plates. Cover with the warm basmati and wild rice pilau. Top with the poached chicken salad and serve.

**Cinnamon**
appetite suppressant, glucose and fat metabolism
**Coriander**
diuretic

# Trattoria-style Superfoods Spelt Flour Margherita Pizza

660 kcal/20g fat

**Makes 4 pizzas**

I originate from Britaly (Bedford), where my reputation clearly now hangs in the balance as I mingle traditional Italian flavours with spelt flour. At least you will be pleased to learn that spelt flour contains considerably more protein than plain flour. So, all being well, you will fill up without filling out.

**For the dough**
**400g white spelt flour, plus extra for dusting**
**2 teaspoons dill seeds**
**¼ teaspoon fine sea salt**
**1 teaspoon sugar**
**½ sachet fast-action dried yeast**
**200ml warm water**
**1 tablespoon olive oil**

**For the pizza sauce**
**200ml passata**
**1 large handful of basil, coarsely chopped**
**1 teaspoon olive oil**
**2 teaspoons dried oregano**
**1 teaspoon dried garlic flakes**
**½ teaspoon dried chilli flakes**
**½ teaspoon freshly ground black pepper**
**½ teaspoon sugar**

**For completing the pizzas**
**3 tomatoes, thinly sliced**
**320g low-fat mozzarella cheese, sliced**
**1 medium red onion, thinly sliced**
**130g shredded low-fat mozzarella cheese (pizza cheese)**
**50g rocket leaves**
**freshly ground black pepper, to taste**

First make the dough. Put all the ingredients into a large mixing bowl and knead for 5 minutes, until you have a firm, elastic dough. The ball needs to be pliable, so you may need to add a few drops of extra water to get the right consistency. Cover the bowl with a clean kitchen towel, put in a warm place and allow the dough to rest for 1 hour.

In the meantime make the pizza sauce by mixing together all of the sauce ingredients in a small bowl. Set aside.

Once the dough has rested, split it into 4 equal portions. Roll each portion between the palms of your hands until you have 4 dough balls. Place each dough ball on a work surface lined with a large sheet of greaseproof paper – one for each dough ball – and flatten into a thick disc. Using a rolling pin, roll into a pizza shape approximately 25cm in diameter. If the dough sticks to the rolling pin, use extra flour for

dusting. Repeat with the other 3 dough balls.

To complete the pizzas, preheat the oven to 220°C/fan 200°C/Gas Mark 7. Spread each pizza base with the prepared sauce, making sure the entire base is covered evenly with the sauce. Layer each pizza with slices of tomato, mozzarella cheese and onion. Top with the shredded mozzarella.

Place one pizza at a time, still on the greaseproof paper, on to a baking tray and bake in the centre of the oven for 12-15 minutes or until crispy. Top with the rocket leaves and season with pepper. Serve immediately.

**Dill**
diuretic, fat metabolism, metabolism booster
**Oregano**
appetite suppressant, fat metabolism
**Chilli**
fat metabolism, metabolism booster
**Black pepper**
fat metabolism, metabolism booster

**Superfood Diet Trattoria-style Spelt Flour Margherita Pizza**
660 kcal/20g fat

**Comparable restaurant-style Margherita pizza**
1912 kcal/74.4g fat

# A Bit On
# The Side

# At a glance...

# Cucumber Salad
50 kcal/4g fat

# My Basic Green Side Salad
55 kcal/4g fat

**Serves 4**

Creamy and aromatic, cucumber is given a whole new dimension here.

**1 tablespoon olive oil**
**1 teaspoon cumin seeds**
**1 teaspoon mustard seeds**
**1 cucumber, peeled, deseeded and thinly sliced**
**1 red chilli, deseeded and finely sliced**
**3 tablespoons chopped fresh coriander**
**2 tablespoons rice vinegar**
**1 tablespoon agave nectar**
**sea salt, to taste**

Pour the olive oil into a deep non-stick pan and add the cumin and mustard seeds. Heat to a high temperature until the seeds start to pop. Remove from the heat and allow to cool.

Once the oil has cooled, combine the remaining ingredients in the pan. Transfer to the refrigerator for a minimum of 1 hour before serving.

**Mustard**
fat metabolism
**Chilli**
fat metabolism, metabolism booster
**Coriander**
diuretic

**Serves 4**

Throw in any other low-calorie vegetables that your heart desires. Cucumber, green beans and peppers are all mighty fine contenders. The calorie content will not go up much and neither will your dress size.

**For the dressing**
**2 tablespoons lemon juice**
**1 teaspoon wholegrain mustard**
**1 teaspoon finely chopped garlic**
**freshly ground black pepper and sea salt, to taste**
**1 tablespoon olive oil**

**For the salad**
**140g mixed salad leaves**
**100g cherry tomatoes**
**1 small red onion, thinly sliced**

In a large salad bowl, combine the lemon juice, mustard, garlic, pepper and salt. Next, mix in the olive oil, making sure it is well combined with the lemon juice.

Add the salad ingredients to the bowl and toss together until well coated in the dressing.

**Mustard**
fat metabolism
**Black pepper**
fat metabolism, metabolism booster

# Hanoi Coleslaw

60 kcal/1.5g fat

**Serves 4**

Fresh coriander and mint add a monumental punch to coleslaw. These wonderfully fragrant herbs also moonlight as natural digestives, which means they help our bodies to digest food efficiently. If that in turn means less gas, and less chance of weight gain, it has to be good news all round.

**For the dressing**
**1 spring onion, thinly sliced**
**1 green chilli (optional), deseeded and thinly sliced**
**2 teaspoons fish sauce**
**3 tablespoons lime juice**
**2 teaspoons agave nectar**
**2 teaspoons rice vinegar**

**For the coleslaw**
**450g cabbage, finely shredded**
**1 carrot, peeled and grated**
**$1/3$ cucumber, halved and sliced**
**1 tablespoon chopped fresh coriander**
**1 tablespoon chopped fresh mint**
**1 tablespoon coarsely chopped peanuts**

Combine all the dressing ingredients in a large bowl. Add all the coleslaw ingredients and toss well to coat in the dressing.

**Chilli**
fat metabolism, metabolism booster
**Coriander**
diuretic

**Superfood Diet Hanoi Coleslaw**
60 kcal/1.5g fat/1110 ORAC units

**Comparable coleslaw**
304 kcal/20g fat/890 ORAC units

# Emperor Beans
80 kcal/4g fat

## Serves 4

Runner beans are a very low-calorie vegetable that you can use regularly. I serve these at room temperature, as the runner beans soak up the sauce while cooling down and becoming deliciously juicy. They can also be served as a satisfying main course for two with a wedge of fresh crusty bread.

**1 tablespoon olive oil**
**1 medium onion, diced**
**2 cloves garlic, sliced**
**2 tomatoes, diced**
**1 carrot, grated**
**250g runner beans, sliced into 6cm lengths**
**1 teaspoon sugar**
**½ teaspoon chilli powder**
**sea salt, to taste**
**1 tablespoon finely chopped fresh dill**

Pour the olive oil into a non-stick pan, add the onion and garlic and cook on a medium heat until the onion is a light brown colour – this should take no longer than 5 minutes. Add the tomatoes and carrot and cook for 5 minutes or until the tomatoes are soft.

Add the runner beans, sugar, chilli powder, salt and 500ml boiling water. Return to the boil. Reduce the heat to a simmer and cook for 20 minutes, uncovered, stirring from time to time. Remove from the heat, stir in the dill, and allow to cool to room temperature before serving.

**Chilli**
fat metabolism, metabolism booster
**Dill**
diuretic, fat metabolism, metabolism booster

# Carrot, Walnut and Quinoa Side Salad
110 kcal/7.5g fat

## Serves 4

Carrots are another of our low-calorie angels that should be dinner-date regulars, and they are perfect partners for walnuts. With the addition of crunchy quinoa, this creamy salad makes a high-end alternative to coleslaw.

**1 red chilli, deseeded and sliced**
**½ clove garlic, crushed**
**1 shallot, finely chopped**
**1 teaspoon mirin**
**1 tablespoon white wine vinegar**
**1 tablespoon chopped fresh coriander**
**1 tablespoon walnut oil**
**350g carrots, grated**
**20g walnuts**
**15g quinoa, cooked according to packet instructions and chilled**
**freshly ground black pepper and sea salt, to taste**
**1 teaspoon poppy seeds**

In a large mixing bowl, combine the chilli, garlic, shallot, mirin, vinegar and coriander. Mix in the walnut oil until thoroughly combined. Add the carrots, walnuts and cooked quinoa. Season to taste with pepper and salt. Refrigerate.

Remove from the refrigerator at least 1 hour before serving. Sprinkle over the poppy seeds just before serving.

**Chilli**
fat metabolism, metabolism booster
**Coriander**
diuretic
**Black pepper**
fat metabolism, metabolism booster

This page: Carrot, Walnut and Quinoa Side Salad, page 159
Right: Roasted Baby Aubergine Salad with Spiced Yogurt Dressing, page 162

**A Bit On The Side**

# Roasted Baby Aubergine Salad with Spiced Yogurt Dressing

120 kcal/9g fat

**Serves 4**

One reason I love aubergine is because it can absorb cooking sauces and dressings so well, almost fooling us into believing it is creating those flavours. Another reason – and not many people know this – is that it contains more nicotine than any other edible plant. Nicotine is a natural appetite suppressant. No wonder aubergine is known in many parts of the world as the 'king of vegetables'. If you prefer, this salad can be served as a main course for two, with fresh crusty bread.

**For the salad**
**8 baby aubergines, halved**
  **lengthways**
**1 tablespoon olive oil**

**For the dressing**
**1 tablespoon olive oil**
**1 teaspoon cumin seeds**
**½ teaspoon turmeric**
**1 clove garlic, crushed**
**1 teaspoon grated fresh root**
  **ginger**
**½ teaspoon dried chilli flakes**
**150g low-fat Greek yogurt**
**sea salt, to taste**
**a handful of pomegranate seeds**
**1 tablespoon coarsely chopped**
  **pistachio nuts**
**1 tablespoon chopped fresh**
  **coriander**

First prepare the aubergines for the salad. Preheat the oven to 240°C/fan 220°C/Gas Mark 9. Brush the cut side of the baby aubergines with the olive oil and place them on a baking tray. Bake in the preheated oven for 15-20 minutes or until the aubergines are light brown in colour. Remove from the oven and allow to cool.

Now make the dressing. Pour the olive oil into a non-stick pan, add the cumin seeds and heat on a high heat until the seeds start to sizzle – this should take no longer than 2-3 minutes. Remove from the heat and quickly mix in the turmeric while the oil is still hot. Allow the oil-and-spice mixture to cool down.

In a mixing bowl, combine the garlic, ginger and chilli flakes with the yogurt. Pour in the cooled oil-and-spice mixture and combine. Add salt to taste.

To assemble the salad, place the roasted aubergine halves on a serving plate and pour over the prepared dressing. Scatter on the pomegranate seeds, pistachio nuts and coriander.

**Turmeric**
fat metabolism
**Ginger**
diuretic, fat metabolism
**Chilli**
fat metabolism, metabolism booster
**Coriander**
diuretic

# Wholegrain Spelt and Seaweed Loaf

130 kcal/2g fat

**Serves 12**

Spelt flour is more nutrient dense than most other traditional baking flours, and often those who are normally intolerant of wheat can eat it. Seaweed is a common ingredient in weight-loss supplements, so try including some in your diet. If you have never baked your own bread, stop loafing around: kneading dough is a great way to de-stress – and nothing beats the aroma of freshly baked bread.

**1 tablespoon olive oil**
**75ml low-fat natural yogurt**
**1 tablespoon agave nectar**
**200ml water**
**400g wholegrain spelt flour, plus extra for dusting**
**2 tablespoons sea salad or 1 sheet of sushi nori, torn into small pieces**
**¼ teaspoon fine sea salt**
**½ sachet fast-action dried yeast**
**2 teaspoons dill seeds**

In a small pan, whisk together the olive oil, yogurt, agave nectar and water. Stir over a low heat until the mixture is warm. (Alternatively, whisk in a bowl, then warm through in a microwave, stirring frequently.)

Place the spelt flour, sea salad or sushi nori, salt, yeast and dill seeds in a large bowl and mix well. Make a well in the middle of this mixture.

Pour the warm yogurt mixture slowly into the well, while stirring with a wooden spoon and gradually mixing in the flour. When the flour is all incorporated, knead for just a few minutes until the dough is smooth and pliable – you may need to add a few drops of water or more flour to get the right consistency. Cover the bowl with a clean kitchen towel and allow the dough to rest for 2 hours.

Turn the dough on to a floured chopping board and knead firmly for several minutes, sprinkling on more flour if required. Shape the dough into a large ball, make 2 diagonal cuts across the top, then dust with some extra flour. Cover the dough and the chopping board with a clean kitchen towel. Leave to rest in a warm place for 30 minutes.

Preheat the oven to 200°C/fan 180°C/Gas Mark 6. Place the dough on a floured baking tray. Bake in the centre of the oven for 35-40 minutes or until the loaf is dark brown in colour. Place the loaf on a wire rack to cool.

**Dill**
diuretic, fat metabolism, metabolism booster

# Super-juicy Watermelon and Feta Salad
140 kcal/6g fat

# Purple Majesty Potato Salad
150kcal/4g fat

**Serves 4**

**Serves 4**

Fruit and cheese together make one of nature's splendid culinary combinations. Watermelon is a prime source of disease-fighting carotenoids, including much-praised lycopene.

**200g low-fat feta cheese, diced**
**500g watermelon, diced**
**1 medium red onion, diced**
**a handful of fresh mint leaves, chopped**
**2 tablespoons balsamic vinegar**
**freshly ground black pepper and sea salt, to taste**

Combine all of the ingredients in a large mixing bowl.

**Black pepper**
fat metabolism, metabolism booster

Try to use purple potatoes here, as they are packed with healthy antioxidants. But if you cannot find them, just use regular potatoes instead.

**500g Purple Majesty potatoes, cut into cubes**
**50g petits pois (fresh or frozen)**
**150g low-fat Greek yogurt**
**1 tablespoon full-fat mayonnaise**
**juice of ½ lemon**
**1 red onion, diced**
**1 clove garlic, finely chopped**
**½ teaspoon dried red chilli flakes (optional)**
**a large handful of fresh basil leaves, chopped**
**a large handful of fresh mint leaves, chopped**
**freshly ground black pepper and sea salt, to taste**

Cook the potatoes in a pan of boiling water until tender. Drain, rinse under cold running water until cool, then drain again and set aside. Cook the petits pois in boiling water for 2-3 minutes, drain and set aside.

Combine the yogurt and mayonnaise in a large mixing bowl until smooth. Mix in the lemon juice. Add the onion, garlic, chilli flakes if using, basil, mint and petits pois, mixing well. Cover and refrigerate for at least 30 minutes.

Combine the potatoes with the yogurt mixture, add seasoning to taste, and serve.

**Chilli**
fat metabolism, metabolism booster
**Black pepper**
fat metabolism, metabolism booster

**Superfood Diet Purple Majesty Potato Salad**
150kcal/4g fat

██████████████████████

**Comparable purple potato salad**
315 kcal/20.6g fat

████████████████████████████████████████████

# Baby Roast Spuds with Rosemary and Turmeric Crust
150 kcal/5g fat

# Easy Chickpeasy Hummus
185 kcal/7g fat

**Serves 6**

**Serves 4**

Research from the University of Texas revealed that turmeric interacts with cells, with an inhibiting effect on weight gain. Perhaps we should take spices a little more seriously: they can do so much more for us than just flavour our food.

**2 tablespoons olive oil**
**½ teaspoon turmeric**
**2 tablespoons finely chopped fresh rosemary leaves**
**sea salt, to taste**
**800g baby new potatoes, halved**

Preheat the oven to 200°C/fan 180°C/Gas Mark 6. In a large bowl combine the olive oil, turmeric, rosemary and salt. Mix through the baby potatoes.

Place the spice-coated potatoes in a single layer on a baking tray. Bake in the centre of the preheated oven for about 25-30 minutes or until golden brown and cooked through, turning once after 15 minutes.

**Turmeric**
fat metabolism
**Rosemary**
diuretic, fat metabolism

Chickpeas contain molybdenum, a trace element that helps build and trigger enzymes involved in repairing and making genetic matter. For now, I hope that you will just enjoy making delicious hummus, knowing that it is doing you good.

**2 x 400g cans chickpeas, rinsed and drained**
**2 cloves garlic, peeled**
**1 green chilli (optional)**
**juice of 2 lemons**
**4 tablespoons low-fat Greek yogurt**
**1 tablespoon sesame oil**
**1 teaspoon freshly ground black pepper**
**sea salt, to taste**
**a large handful of fresh coriander leaves**
**cucumber, carrot and celery sticks, to serve**

Place all the ingredients in a food processor and blend until a smooth, light, mousse-like texture is attained. Serve the hummus with vegetable sticks.

Store in an airtight container in the refrigerator for up to 3 days.

**Chilli**
fat metabolism, metabolism booster
**Black pepper**
fat metabolism, metabolism booster
**Coriander**
diuretic

**Superfood Diet Baby Roast Spuds with Rosemary and Turmeric Crust**
150 kcal/5g fat/4050 ORAC units

**Comparable Roast Potatoes**
290 kcal/10.6g fat/2080 ORAC units

Left: Wholegrain Spelt and Seaweed Loaf, page 163
This page: Baby Roast Spuds with Rosemary and Turmeric Crust, page 165

**A Bit On The Side**

# Roasted Okra
185 kcal/12g fat

**Serves 4**

Okra is a natural diuretic. Handy if you happen to be a featherweight boxer. If you have never tried okra, sadly you will not know what you are missing. It is a knockout. Spiced and roasted, it makes a perfect side dish — but also doubles as a light meal if wrapped in a flatbread.

**500g okra, stalks removed**
**3 tablespoons olive oil**
**2 cloves garlic, sliced**
**½ teaspoon turmeric**
**sea salt, to taste**
**1 teaspoon sugar**
**1 green chilli, finely chopped**
**1 tablespoon finely grated fresh**
   **root ginger**
**400ml passata**
**2 tablespoons light coconut milk**
   **(optional)**
**chopped fresh coriander,**
   **to garnish**

Preheat the oven to 200°C/fan 180°C/Gas Mark 6. In a large mixing bowl, toss the okra in 2 tablespoons of the olive oil and transfer to a baking tray.

Roast the okra in the centre of the preheated oven for 15-20 minutes or until the pods are just tender.

Meanwhile, heat the remaining 1 tablespoon of olive oil in a non-stick pan, add the garlic and cook over a low-medium heat until the garlic turns a golden brown colour, stirring all the time – this should take no more than 2 minutes. Add the turmeric, salt and sugar, mix well and cook for 20 seconds. Finally, add the chilli, ginger, passata and coconut milk, if using. Bring the sauce to a simmer and cook for 5 minutes.

Mix the roasted okra through the sauce and heat through for 2 minutes. Garnish with coriander before serving.

**Turmeric**
fat metabolism
**Chilli**
fat metabolism, metabolism booster
**Ginger**
diuretic, fat metabolism
**Coriander**
diuretic

# Superfoods Gluten-free Tabbouleh
235 kcal/6g fat

**Serves 4**

In this salad, we swap bulgur wheat for quinoa and with this simple barter we lose the gluten. The payoff is quite literally a finer salad.

**For the salad**
**50g petits pois (fresh or frozen)**
**80g broad beans (fresh or frozen)**
**120g quinoa, cooked according to packet instructions and chilled**
**70g Puy lentils, cooked according to packet instructions and chilled**
**1 small red onion, diced**
**1 spring onion, finely chopped**
**2 tablespoons chopped flat-leaf parsley**
**1 tablespoon chopped fresh mint**

**For the dressing**
**juice of 2 lemons**
**1 clove garlic, crushed**
**1 tablespoon olive oil**
**freshly ground black pepper and sea salt, to taste**

Cook the petits pois in boiling water for 2-3 minutes, drain and leave to cool. Cook the broad beans in boiling water for 3-5 minutes or until tender, drain and leave to cool.

In a large salad bowl, combine the petits pois, broad beans, quinoa, lentils, red onion, spring onion, parsley and mint.

To make the dressing, combine the lemon juice and crushed garlic in a small bowl and mix in the olive oil. Add seasoning to taste.

Pour the dressing over the quinoa mixture and thoroughly combine. Cover and refrigerate for at least 1 hour before serving.

**Parsley**
diuretic, fat metabolism
**Black pepper**
fat metabolism, metabolism booster

# Crazy Purple Mash

145 kcal/0.5g fat

# Parsnip and Sweet Potato Mash

155 kcal/0.5g fat

# Rosemary Mash

160 kcal/0.5g fat

**Serves 4**

**Serves 4**

**Serves 4**

**1kg Purple Majesty potatoes**
**50ml semi-skimmed milk**
**1 teaspoon garlic powder**
**sea salt, to taste**

Peel the potatoes and cut into even-sized pieces. Boil them in plenty of water until soft. Drain, then mash, using a potato-masher. Mix in the milk, garlic powder and salt.

**400g parsnips, peeled and diced**
**500g sweet potatoes, peeled and**
   **diced**
**1 clove garlic, crushed**
**50ml quark (skimmed milk soft**
   **cheese)**
**a pinch of ground nutmeg**
**3 tablespoons chopped fresh**
   **chives**
**freshly ground black pepper and**
   **sea salt, to taste**

Steam the parsnips and sweet potatoes until soft. Place the steamed vegetables in a large mixing bowl. Add the garlic, and mash until smooth. Mix through the remaining ingredients.

**1kg potatoes**
**50ml semi-skimmed milk**
**½ tablespoon fresh rosemary**
   **leaves, finely chopped**
**sea salt, to taste**

Peel the potatoes and cut into even-sized pieces. Boil them in plenty of water until soft. Drain, then mash, using a potato-masher. Mix in the milk, rosemary and salt.

**Rosemary**
diuretic, fat metabolism

# Mustard Mash
175 kcal/1g fat

# Horseradish Mash
180 kcal/1g fat

Serves 4

Serves 4

**1kg potatoes**
**4 tablespoons low-fat Greek**
  **yogurt**
**1 tablespoon English mustard**
**sea salt, to taste**

Peel the potatoes and cut into even-sized pieces. Boil them in plenty of water until soft. Drain, then mash, using a potato-masher. Mix in the yogurt, mustard and salt.

**Mustard**
fat metabolism

**1kg potatoes**
**2 tablespoons low-fat Greek**
  **yogurt**
**2 tablespoons horseradish sauce**
**sea salt, to taste**

Peel the potatoes and cut into even-sized pieces. Boil them in plenty of water until soft. Drain, then mash, using a potato-masher. Mix in the yogurt, horseradish sauce and salt.

# Sushi Rice Pilau

165 kcal/fat neg

# Basmati and Wild Rice Pilau

175 kcal/fat neg

# Basmati Rice Pilau

175 kcal/fat neg

**Serves 4**

**200g sushi rice**
**400ml boiling water**

Place the ingredients in a large, microwave-safe bowl and mix with a fork. Microwave, uncovered, for 4 minutes on HIGH at 700W, or for 3½ minutes on HIGH at 800W or for 3 minutes on HIGH at 900W.

Mix with a fork. Microwave, uncovered, for a further 4 minutes on HIGH at 700W, or for a further 3½ minutes on HIGH at 800W, or for a further 3 minutes on HIGH at 900W.

Mix with a fork. Microwave, uncovered for a further 4 minutes on HIGH at 700W, or for a further 3½ minutes on HIGH at 800W, or for a further 3 minutes on HIGH at 900W.

Take the pilau out of the microwave, mix with a fork and leave to stand, uncovered, for 10 minutes. Fluff the rice with a fork and serve.

**Serves 4**

**200g basmati and wild rice**
**400ml boiling water**

Follow instructions for Sushi Rice Pilau, left.

**Serves 4**

**200g basmati rice**
**400ml boiling water**

Place the ingredients in a large microwave-safe bowl and mix with a fork. Microwave, uncovered, for 4 minutes on HIGH at 700W, or for 3½ minutes on HIGH at 800W or for 3 minutes on HIGH at 900W.

Mix with a fork. Microwave, uncovered, for a further 4 minutes on HIGH at 700W, or for a further 3½ minutes on HIGH at 800W, or for a further 3 minutes on HIGH at 900W.

Mix with a fork. Cover the bowl and microwave for a further 4 minutes on HIGH at 700W, or for a further 3½ minutes on HIGH at 800W, or for a further 3 minutes on HIGH at 900W.

Take the pilau out of the microwave and leave to stand, covered, for 10 minutes. Fluff the rice with a fork and serve.

**The Superfood Diet**

# Cardamom Pilau
175 kcal/fat neg

# Brown Rice Pilau
180 kcal/1.5g fat

# Toasted Brown Rice
180 kcal/1.5g fat

**Serves 4**

**Serves 4**

**Serves 4**

Follow recipe for Basmati Rice Pilau, but add 10 green cardamom pods, lightly crushed, at the beginning, before cooking.

Cumin Pilau
Follow recipe for Basmati Rice Pilau, but add 1 teaspoon cumin seeds at the beginning, before cooking.

Garlic Pilau
Follow recipe for Basmati Rice Pilau, but add 1 tablespoon dried garlic flakes at the beginning, before cooking.

**200g brown rice, washed and drained**
**1.5 litres boiling water**

Place the rice in a deep saucepan and pour over the water. Return to the boil and cook on a medium-high heat, uncovered, for 30 minutes. Use a large spoon to skim any foam that rises to the surface.

Turn the rice into a large sieve to drain, pour through fresh boiling water, drain again and return to the pan. Lay 2 sheets of kitchen paper over the rice to absorb the steam, cover the pan and leave to stand for 5 minutes before serving.

Totally addictive.

**Brown Rice Pilau (see left), a day old and chilled**

Preheat the oven to 180°C/fan 160°C/Gas Mark 4.

Spread the rice in an even layer on a baking tray and bake in the centre of the oven for 20-25 minutes or until crisp, mixing the rice once after 15 minutes.

**The Superfood Diet**

# Jasmine Rice Pilau
195 kcal/fat neg

# Superfoods Goji Berry and Green Pea Pilau
220 kcal/3g fat

**Serves 4**

**Serves 4**

**200g jasmine rice**
**450ml boiling water**

Follow instructions for Basmati Rice Pilau on page 174.

Goji berries contain almost twice as much vitamin C as oranges. Calcium is absorbed by your body more efficiently when you eat foods rich in vitamin C, and calcium aids with weight loss. Complicated, I know. Just keep eating.

**½ tablespoon olive oil**
**1 stick of cinnamon**
**1 teaspoon cumin seeds**
**1 carrot, grated**
**200g basmati and wild rice**
**sea salt, to taste**
**375ml boiling water**
**a small handful of dried goji**
**    berries**
**a handful of green peas**
**    (fresh or frozen)**

Pour the olive oil into a non-stick frying pan, add the cinnamon stick and cumin seeds and cook over a low-medium heat until the seeds begin to pop – this should take no more than 2–3 minutes.

Place the fried cinnamon and cumin, carrot, basmati and wild rice, salt and boiling water in a large microwave-safe bowl and mix with a fork.

Microwave, uncovered, for 4 minutes on HIGH at 700W, or for 3½ minutes on HIGH at 800W or for 3 minutes on HIGH at 900W.

Mix with a fork. Microwave, uncovered, for a further 4 minutes on HIGH at 700W, or for a further 3½ minutes on HIGH at 800W, or for a further 3 minutes on HIGH at 900W.

Mix with a fork. Microwave, uncovered, for a further 4 minutes on HIGH at 700W, or for a further 3½ minutes on HIGH at 800W, or for a further 3 minutes on HIGH at 900W.

Take the pilau out of the microwave. Scatter the goji berries and peas on top of the rice, cover and leave to stand for 10 minutes. Fluff the rice with a fork and serve.

**Cinnamon**
appetite suppressant, glucose and fat metabolism

5

# Have Your Cake and Eat It

# At a glance...

# Almost Fat-free Strawberries and Ginger-infused Yogurt

## 115 kcal/0.5 g fat

**Serves 4**

Incredibly, the only fat in this recipe comes from the strawberries.
So you can enjoy them free of guilt – and just think of all the good things that those lovely antioxidants are doing.

**500g Fage Total 0% fat Greek yogurt**
**2 tablespoons stem ginger syrup**
**20g stem ginger, diced**
**400g strawberries, sliced**
**½ teaspoon ground cinnamon**
**a handful of fresh mint leaves, finely chopped**

In a medium-sized bowl, combine the yogurt with the stem ginger syrup, then mix in the diced stem ginger. Divide the yogurt mixture equally between 4 bowls and top with the strawberries. Dust with cinnamon and top with chopped mint.

**Ginger**
diuretic, fat metabolism
**Cinnamon**
appetite suppressant, glucose and fat metabolism

# Superfoods Vitamin C Energy Balls

120 kcal/4.5g fat

**Serves 8**

Keep these high-energy snacks on standby for whenever you need a pick-me-up or healthy treat.

**75g unsalted cashew nuts**
**¼ teaspoon ground ginger or cinnamon, or to taste**
**90g dried goji berries**
**85g dates, stoned and chopped**
**½ -1 tablespoon grapefruit juice (optional), chilled**

Place the cashew nuts and ginger or cinnamon in a food processor and blitz until the nuts resemble fine breadcrumbs. Add the dried fruits to the food processor and process until the mixture has formed a paste. You may need to add a few drops of grapefruit juice to get the right consistency.

Divide the mixture into 8 equal portions. Using the palms of your hands, shape each portion into a ball. Cover each ball with cling film and chill in the refrigerator before serving.

**Ginger**
diuretic, fat metabolism
**Cinnamon**
appetite suppressant, glucose and fat metabolism

# Superfruit Cake

## 130 kcal/0.5g fat

**Serves 30**

Made up almost entirely of fruit, and combined with just enough rye flour to bind it all together, this is clearly a most natural and low-fat cake. As with any dense fruit cake, keep the portions small.

**900g dried mixed fruit**
**50g dried goji berries**
**2 teaspoons ground ginger**
**1 teaspoon ground cinnamon**
**500ml green tea, cooled**
**350g rye flour**
**1 teaspoon baking powder**
**1 teaspoon bicarbonate of soda**

Place the dried mixed fruit, goji berries, ginger and cinnamon in a large non-metallic mixing bowl. Pour the green tea over the fruit and mix well. Cover and allow to rest overnight.

Preheat the oven to 140°C/ fan 120°C/Gas Mark 1. Line a deep round 23cm cake tin with greaseproof paper and set aside.

Stir the rye flour, baking powder and bicarbonate of soda into the bowl of mixed fruit until it is combined thoroughly and turn the mixture into the centre of the cake tin. Using the back of a spoon, push the mixture out to the sides of the cake tin until even.

Bake at the bottom of the oven for 2–2½ hours or until the cake is cooked through – it should feel firm, and a skewer sunk into the centre should come out clean. Leave to cool in the tin for 10 minutes, then turn out on to a wire rack, cover with a clean kitchen towel, and leave to cool completely.

**Ginger**
diuretic, fat metabolism
**Cinnamon**
appetite suppressant, glucose and fat metabolism

**Superfood Diet Superfruit Cake**
130 kcal/0.5g fat/1215 ORAC units

**Comparable fruit cake**
350 kcal/8g fat/1020 ORAC units

The Superfood Diet

# Virtuoso Tiramisu

## 170 kcal/2g fat

**Serves 6**

Above and beyond anything else, tiramisu is my pudding of choice. Swapping mascarpone and cream for quark and fat-free Greek yogurt was one of those nerve-wracking culinary experiments I shall not be forgetting for a while. I think it works.

**40g cocoa powder**
**½ teaspoon ground cinnamon**
**250g quark (skimmed milk soft cheese)**
**250g Fage Total 0% fat Greek yogurt**
**1 teaspoon vanilla extract**
**5 tablespoons agave nectar**
**4 tablespoons Kahlúa**
**250ml espresso coffee, chilled**
**16 large sponge finger biscuits (preferably Italian savoiardi)**

In a small bowl, combine the cocoa powder and ground cinnamon. Set aside. In a large bowl, combine the quark, yogurt, vanilla extract, agave nectar and Kahlúa. Pour the chilled coffee into a separate, shallow bowl.

Dip 8 sponge fingers into the coffee, one at a time, and place them in a row at the bottom of a rectangular dish. Spread half of the quark and yogurt mixture on top of the soaked sponge fingers and sprinkle over half of the cocoa-cinnamon powder.

Dip the remaining 8 sponge fingers in the coffee and place them on top of the first layer in the rectangular dish. Spread the remaining quark and yogurt mixture on top and finish by sprinkling over the remaining cocoa-cinnamon powder.

Refrigerate for 2 hours before serving.

**Cinnamon**
appetite suppressant, glucose and fat metabolism

**Superfood Diet Virtuoso Tiramisu**
170 kcal/2g fat/3930 ORAC units

**Comparable tiramisu**
602 kcal/45.8g fat/3710 ORAC units

# Saffron Pears with Blueberries and Pistachios

## 170 kcal/2.5g fat

**Serves 4**

Only natural ingredients here. Not a smidgen of anything processed. Still, this is one heck of an indulgent-tasting pudding.

**8 firm pears, peeled, cored and quartered**
**1 teaspoon finely grated lemon rind**
**4 green cardamom pods, lightly crushed**
**a pinch of saffron**
**200g low-fat Greek yogurt**
**200g blueberries**
**1 tablespoon coarsely chopped pistachio nuts**

Place the pear quarters, lemon rind, cardamoms and saffron with 1 tablespoon water in a saucepan. Cover and cook over a low heat, stirring from time to time, for approximately 10 minutes or until the pears are soft. Remove from the heat and allow to cool, then discard the cardamoms. Turn the pears into a bowl and refrigerate until chilled.

Spoon the pears into 4 serving bowls. Top each bowl with yogurt, blueberries and pistachios.

# Amaretti, Blueberry and Chocolate Trifle

## 170 kcal/4g fat

**Serves 1**

A lazy but luscious dessert for one, for when you cannot be bothered to cook.

**15g amaretti biscuits**
**100g low-fat Greek yogurt**
**50g blueberries**
**5g dark chocolate, grated**
**a pinch of ground cinnamon**

Place the biscuits at the bottom of a dessert glass and spoon in the yogurt. Top with the blueberries, then finish with a dusting of chocolate and cinnamon. Refrigerate for 1 hour before serving.

**Cinnamon**
appetite suppressant, glucose and fat metabolism

# Chocolate and Chilli Raspberry Cheesecake

220 kcal/7g fat

**Serves 10**

It comes as no surprise to learn that most of the fat and calories in traditional cheesecake are to be found in the filling. With this Superfood Diet recipe you will be making an almost fat-free version, using quark and fat-free Greek yogurt. You do pick up a smidgen of fat in the base, but it is coconut oil, which is proven to burn fat in your body by increasing the metabolic rate.

**For the base**
**65g white spelt flour**
**40g rolled oats**
**¼ teaspoon baking powder**
**75g dark brown soft sugar**
**50g coconut oil, melted**

**For the filling**
**6 leaves gelatine**
**150ml semi-skimmed milk**
**50g cocoa powder**
**1 teaspoon ground cinnamon**
**¼ teaspoon chilli powder**
**5 tablespoons agave nectar**
**500g quark (skimmed milk soft cheese)**
**300g Fage Total 0% fat Greek yogurt**
**1 teaspoon vanilla extract**
**2 egg whites**
**300g raspberries**

First make the base. Preheat the oven to 200°C/fan 180°C/Gas Mark 6. Line a 23cm springform tin with greaseproof paper. In a large bowl, combine the flour, oats, baking powder, sugar and coconut oil. Mix into a fine crumble, using your fingertips. Pat the mixture firmly into the tin.

Bake the base in the centre of the oven for 20-25 minutes, or until golden brown. Remove from the oven and allow to cool.

To make the filling, soak the gelatine leaves in a bowl of cold water for 10 minutes. Put the milk, cocoa powder, cinnamon, chilli powder and agave nectar into a milk pan. Bring to a simmer on a medium heat, stirring frequently, until the cocoa and milk are combined. Remove from the heat and leave to cool for a few minutes. Remove the soaked gelatine leaves from the water, whisk them into the cocoa mixture and set aside.

Place the quark and yogurt in a large mixing bowl and whisk together until smooth. Add the vanilla extract and mix. Add the cocoa mixture. Beat until smooth and set aside.

In a separate bowl, whisk the egg whites until soft peaks form. Slowly fold the egg whites into the quark and yogurt mixture.

Spoon the filling mixture on to the base. Refrigerate overnight to set. Top with the raspberries before serving.

**Cinnamon**
appetite suppressant, glucose and fat metabolism
**Chilli**
fat metabolism, metabolism booster

**Superfood Diet Chocolate and Chilli Raspberry Cheesecake**
220 kcal/7g fat/1800 ORAC units

**Comparable cheesecake**
762kcal/56.4g fat/ORAC units neg

# Chilled Mango, Banana and Raspberry Soup

250 kcal/6g fat

**Serves 4**

Researchers at the University of Queensland have pointed to mango as an aid to counteract weight gain. Banana is the taste of childhood, while raspberries and mango have a more sophisticated feel about them. It's like having a whole fruity family in a bowl.

**400ml mango pulp, chilled**
**500g low-fat Greek yogurt**
**1 banana, diced into small cubes**
**2 passion fruits, halved, pulp and seeds scooped out**
**80g raspberries**
**15g toasted flaked almonds**
**a few fresh mint leaves**

Combine the mango pulp, yogurt, banana, and passion fruit pulp and seeds in a large bowl. Refrigerate for 1 hour.

To serve, divide the soup equally between 4 serving bowls. Top with the raspberries, and scatter over the flaked almonds and mint leaves.

# Gluten-free Orange Cake

255 kcal/16g fat

**Serves 16**

This Spanish-inspired cake needs little by way of introduction. It is as simple to make as it is delicious to eat. Scientists at the City of Hope National Medical Center in California advocate an almond-enriched diet to encourage weight reduction.

**2 medium oranges**
**7 eggs**
**200g light brown soft sugar**
**370g ground almonds**
**½ teaspoon ground cinnamon**
**30g flaked almonds**

Place the whole oranges in a deep saucepan and cover with boiling water. Return the water to the boil, then reduce to a simmer, cover and cook for 1 hour. Remove the oranges carefully from the water, place them in a bowl of iced water and leave to cool. Cut them into quarters and blitz in a food processor. Set aside.

Preheat the oven to 180°C/ fan 160°C/Gas Mark 4. Line a deep round 23cm cake tin with greaseproof paper. In a large mixing bowl, beat the eggs and sugar until thoroughly combined and creamy in texture. Add the puréed oranges, ground almonds and cinnamon. Mix well.

Pour the mixture into the cake tin and sprinkle over the flaked almonds. Bake in the centre of the oven for 1 hour 20 minutes.

**Cinnamon**
appetite suppressant, glucose and fat metabolism

**Superfood Diet Gluten-free Orange Cake**
255 kcal/16g fat/1720 ORAC units

**Comparable orange and almond cake**
600.9kcal/28.2g fat/1640 ORAC units

This page: Chocolate and Chilli Raspberry Cheesecake, page 191
Right: Gluten-free Orange Cake, page 193

# Refreshments

# At a glance...

## Cuppas

## Smoothies

# Happy Hour

**206 Masala Vodka**
55 kcal/fat neg

**206 Galliano-style Vodka**
55 kcal/fat neg

**206 Masala Mary**
80 kcal/fat neg

**207 Pink Fizz**
105 kcal/0.5g fat

**207 Harvey Wallbanger**
105 kcal/fat neg

**207 Cinnamon Champagne Cocktail**
140 kcal/fat neg

**210 Hangover-prevention Cocktail**
350 kcal/0.5g fat

**210 Smokin' Almonds**
75 kcal/6.5g fat

**210 Chilli Pineapple**
90 kcal/0.5g fat

# Healing Brews

**The Superfood Diet**

## Energising Black Coffee with Lemon

**Serves 1**

If this does not wake you up and kick off your day, nothing else really will. But remember to use level teaspoons, not heaped!

**2 teaspoons instant coffee**
**1 green cardamom pod, lightly crushed**
**1 slice of lemon**

Place the coffee, cardamom and lemon slice in a cup. Pour over boiling water and mix well.

Cover and allow to stand for 5 minutes before drinking.

## Chai for One

**Serves 1**

You can save a fortune by making your own masala chai (spiced tea).

**1 black tea bag**
**1 green cardamom pod, lightly crushed**
**milk and sugar, to taste**

Place the tea bag and cardamom in a mug. Pour over the boiling water. Cover and leave to brew for 5 minutes. Remove the tea bag. Add milk and sugar to taste.

## Chai Green Tea

**Serves 3**

Total calories depend on how much honey you use. Without honey, this tea is virtually calorie-free.

**1 green tea bag**
**1 stick of cinnamon**
**2 green cardamom pods, lightly crushed**
**a large pinch of ground ginger**
**a pinch of saffron**
**clear honey (optional), to taste**

Place the tea bag, cinnamon stick, cardamoms, ginger and saffron, and a squeeze of honey, if using, in a saucepan. Add 3 mugs (900ml) cold water to the pan, and bring to the boil. Reduce to a low heat, cover and simmer gently for 10 minutes.

Remove the pan from the heat. Discard the tea bag and strain the tea into mugs.

**Cinnamon**
appetite suppressant, glucose and fat metabolism
**Ginger**
diuretic, fat metabolism

# Fig and Peach Smoothie

60 kcal/fat neg

**Serves 2**

Buddha found nirvana under a fig tree. I like to think I reached my own transcendental state by producing a smoothie from the fruit. Green and earthy-tasting, with a minimal calorie and fat content, this smoothie is perfectly in sync with the Buddhist ethos.

**3 figs**
**1 peach, stoned**
**15g baby spinach leaves**
**a pinch of ground cinnamon**
**225ml cold water**
**a large handful of ice, plus extra to serve**

Put all the ingredients into a blender and blitz until smooth. Place the extra ice in 2 tall glasses and pour in the smoothie. Serve immediately.

**Cinnamon**
appetite suppressant, glucose and fat metabolism

# Watermelon, Ginger and Mint Smoothie

65 kcal/0.5g fat

**Serves 2**

Watermelon is 91 per cent water. Hence the modest calorie count. Extreme refreshment – just right for a hot summer's day.

**450g watermelon, diced**
**1 teaspoon lime juice**
**1 teaspoon finely grated fresh root ginger**
**10 fresh mint leaves, plus extra to decorate**
**a large handful of ice, plus extra to serve**

Put all the ingredients into a blender and blitz until smooth. Place the extra ice in 2 tall glasses and pour in the smoothie. Decorate each glass with a few extra mint leaves and serve immediately.

**Ginger**
diuretic, fat metabolism

# Strawberry and Mint Smoothie

100 kcal/2g fat

**Serves 2**

Berries, notably strawberries, are linked to weight loss. I cannot imagine a more delicious way to take in 100 calories.

**250g strawberries**
**a few fresh mint leaves, plus extra to decorate**
**200ml low-fat natural yogurt**
**a large handful of ice, plus extra to serve**

Put all the ingredients into a blender and blitz until smooth. Place the extra ice in 2 tall glasses and pour in the smoothie. Decorate each glass with a few extra mint leaves and serve immediately.

# Apple and Grape Smoothie

105 kcal/1g fat

**Serves 2**

An apple a day really does help to keep the doctor away! Fibre-rich apples are linked to weight loss and can help to protect against cancer. Fresh root ginger gives this smoothie a clean, refreshing taste – but cinnamon also works beautifully with apples, so I recommend you try that combination too.

**1 apple, peeled and cored**
**170g grapes**
**30g baby spinach leaves**
**1 teaspoon finely grated fresh**
  **root ginger or a pinch of ground**
  **cinnamon**
**125ml cold water**
**a large handful of ice, plus extra**
  **to serve**

Put all the ingredients into a blender and blitz until smooth. Place the extra ice in 2 tall glasses and pour in the smoothie. Serve immediately.

**Ginger**
diuretic, fat metabolism

# Banana and Almond Smoothie

120 kcal/3g fat

**Serves 1**

Containing just one third of the calories of skimmed milk, almond milk is a mere shadow of its dairy cousin. Still, it manages to squeeze in more nutrients than any other dairy-milk alternative. Paired with banana, it makes a smoothie that sure beats a powdered diet shake. To ensure a thick and creamy texture, freeze the banana first.

**100g banana, frozen and cut into**
  **pieces**
**250ml unsweetened almond milk**
**a pinch of ground cinnamon**
**a large handful of ice, plus extra**
  **to serve**

Put all the ingredients into a blender and blitz until smooth. Place the extra ice in a tall glass and pour in the smoothie. Serve immediately.

**Cinnamon**
appetite suppressant, glucose and fat metabolism

**The Superfood Diet**

# Mango, Passion Fruit and Ginger Smoothie

145 kcal/3g fat

**Serves 2**

There is significant evidence that mangoes are packed with weight-reducing agents. This is particularly true of West African varieties. Anyone for a mango hunt?

**175g prepared mango flesh, diced**
**1 passion fruit, halved, pulp and**
**seeds scooped out**
**1 teaspoon finely grated fresh**
**root ginger**
**300ml low-fat natural yogurt**
**a large handful of ice, plus extra**
**to serve**

Put all the ingredients into a blender and blitz until smooth. Place the extra ice in 2 tall glasses and pour in the smoothie. Serve immediately.

**Ginger**
diuretic, fat metabolism

# Blueberry and Banana Smoothie

150 kcal/2g fat

**Serves 3**

Insulin is essential for regulating blood sugar but, with too much of it, our bodies have trouble burning up fat. Insulin resistance, which develops in obese men and women, only causes the body to produce yet more insulin. Blueberries might come to the rescue here. According to research conducted at Louisiana State University, 'bioactives in blueberries improve insulin sensitivity in obese, insulin-resistant men and women'.

**300g blueberries**
**1 banana**
**100ml apple juice**
**300ml low-fat natural yogurt**
**1 teaspoon finely grated fresh**
**root ginger**
**a large handful of ice, plus extra**
**to serve**

Put all the ingredients into a blender and blitz until smooth. Place the extra ice in 3 tall glasses and pour in the smoothie. Serve immediately.

**Ginger**
diuretic, fat metabolism

# Masala Vodka
55 kcal/fat neg

# Galliano-style Vodka
55 kcal/fat neg

# Masala Mary
80 kcal/fat neg

**Makes 28 shots**

**Makes 28 shots**

**Serves 1**

**700ml good-quality vodka**
**2 sticks of cinnamon**
**20 green cardamom pods, lightly
  crushed**
**10 cloves**

Pour the vodka into a clean,
1 litre glass bottle or jar. Add all the
spices and seal or close the bottle
or jar. Place in a cool, dark place
overnight.

The next day, strain the infused
vodka back into its original bottle,
seal and use as required.

**700ml good-quality vodka**
**2 vanilla pods**
**2 star anise**
**10 dried juniper berries**
**6 fresh root ginger batons,
  roughly same size as
  matchsticks**
**2 teaspoons finely grated lemon
  rind**

Pour the vodka into a clean,
1 litre glass bottle or jar. Add all the
remaining ingredients and seal or
close the bottle or jar. Store in a
cool, dark place until required.

Masala spices lift the traditional
Bloody Mary, giving it an extra zap
and creating the perfect pick-me-
up.

**a large handful of ice**
**25ml Masala Vodka (see recipe
  left)**
**125ml vegetable or tomato juice**
**Worcestershire sauce, to taste**
**Tabasco sauce, to taste**
**white pepper, to taste**
**1 stick of celery, to serve**

Place the ice in a tall glass and
pour on the masala vodka. Pour
in the vegetable or tomato juice,
then add a good slug of both
Worcestershire and Tabasco sauces,
and a sprinkling of pepper. Stir well
and serve garnished with the celery
stick.

**The Superfood Diet**

# Pink Fizz
105 kcal/0.5g fat

# Harvey Wallbanger
105 kcal/fat neg

# Cinnamon Champagne Cocktail
140 kcal/fat neg

**Serves 2**

Sitting merrily between Pimms and Bucks Fizz, this cocktail ticks quite a few boxes.

**400g watermelon, diced**
**125ml Champagne or dry**
    **sparkling wine**
**a few fresh mint leaves, plus extra**
    **to decorate**
**a large handful of ice, plus extra**
    **to serve**

Put all the ingredients into a blender and blitz until smooth. Place the extra ice in 2 tall glasses and pour in the cocktail. Decorate each glass with a few extra mint leaves and serve immediately.

**Serves 1**

Instead of calorific Galliano liqueur I've used my own spice-infused vodka which, I think you will agree, has remarkably similar flavours.

**a large handful of ice**
**25ml Galliano-style Vodka**
    **(see page 206)**
**125ml orange juice**
**1 slice of orange**

Place the ice in a tall glass and pour on the Galliano-style vodka. Pour in the orange juice and stir well. Top with the slice of orange.

**Serves 1**

I call this a Champagne cocktail, but why waste of a good bottle of bubbly when a standard sparkling wine will do just as well here? The splash of cinnamon syrup will transform it into something spectacular.

**1 tablespoon cinnamon syrup,**
    **chilled**
**125ml sparkling wine, chilled**

Pour the sparkling wine into a Champagne flute and drizzle the cinnamon syrup over the top.

Left: Hangover-prevention Cocktail, page 210
This page: Cinnamon Champagne Cocktail, page 207

**Refreshments**

# Hangover-prevention Cocktail

350 kcal/0.5g fat

**Serves 1**

My headlining, vodka-based cocktail contains analgesic and digestive spices, as well as acai juice, which repairs some of the free-radical damage caused by alcohol. Think of it as drinking a cocktail come natural Alka-Seltzer the night before the day after!

**a large handful of ice**
**a few fresh mint leaves**
**25ml Masala Vodka (see page 206)**
**15ml Cointreau**
**30ml acai juice (available from health-food shops)**
**330ml pomegranate-based smoothie or pomegranate juice**
**1 stick of cinnamon**

Place the ice in a tall glass and sprinkle in a few mint leaves. Pour in the masala vodka, Cointreau and acai juice. Top up with the pomegranate-based smoothie or pomegranate juice, and stir well. Decorate with the cinnamon stick and serve.

# Smokin' Almonds

75 kcal/6.5g fat

**Serves 25**

Scientists at the City of Hope National Medical Center in California monitored two groups, to evaluate the weight-loss effect of an almond-enriched diet against a high-carb, low-calorie regime. They found that, 'the almond group experienced a sustained and greater weight reduction for the duration'. These nuts combine so well with the Chilli Pineapple (see right).

**300g unblanched almonds**
**1 tablespoon fresh rosemary leaves**
**1 teaspoon smoked paprika**
**½ teaspoon dried chilli flakes**
**½ teaspoon freshly ground black pepper**
**sea salt, to taste**
**1 tablespoon olive oil**

Preheat the oven to 200°C/fan 180°C/Gas Mark 6. Place the almonds and rosemary on a baking tray in the centre of the oven for 7 minutes or until the almonds have developed a fragrant aroma. In a large bowl meanwhile, mix together the paprika, chilli, pepper, salt and olive oil. Add the almonds and rosemary to the bowl and toss until well coated. Set aside to cool. Store in an airtight container. Serve the required amount into a shallow dish. I have allowed for 10 almonds (2 small handfuls per serving).

**Rosemary**
diuretic, fat metabolism
**Chilli and black pepper**
fat metabolism, metabolism boosters

# Chilli Pineapple

90 kcal/0.5g fat

**Serves 5**

Pineapple contains bromelain, an enzyme which breaks down protein and aids digestion. For me this is less of a recipe. More fetish. Love at first bite.

**150g dried pineapple chunks**
**½ teaspoon chilli powder**

Combine the ingredients in a bowl, tossing the pineapple chunks until they are well coated in the chilli. Store in an airtight container and use as required, within 1 month.

**Chilli**
fat metabolism, metabolism booster

**The Superfood Diet**

**The Superfood Diet**

# Appetite-suppressant Diet Tea

**Serves 3**

Cinnamon is known to assist with glucose metabolism, helping to lower blood sugar levels. For a dieter, this means less hunger.

**1 green tea bag**
**2 sticks of cinnamon**
**1 tablespoon fennel seeds**
**1 large pinch of ground ginger**

Place the tea bag, cinnamon sticks, fennel seeds and ginger in a saucepan. Add 3 mugs (900ml) cold water to the pan, and bring to the boil. Reduce to a low heat, cover and simmer gently for 10 minutes.

Remove the pan from the heat. Discard the tea bag and strain the tea into mugs.

**Cinnamon**
appetite suppressant, glucose and fat metabolism
**Fennel**
appetite suppressant
**Ginger**
diuretic, fat metabolism

# Soothing Cough-and-Cold Tea

**Serves 3**

Cinnamon, with honey, is an age-old remedy for coughs and sore throats. Recent research into cinnamon oil has revealed the many ways in which it comes to the rescue.

**1 green tea bag**
**2 sticks of cinnamon**
**5 green cardamom pods, lightly**
**  crushed**
**a large pinch of ground ginger**
**a large pinch of saffron**
**3 tablespoons clear honey**

Place the tea bag, cinnamon sticks, cardamoms, ginger, saffron and honey in a saucepan. Add 3 mugs (900ml) cold water to the pan, and bring to the boil. Reduce to a low heat, cover and simmer gently for 10 minutes.

Remove the pan from the heat. Discard the tea bag and strain the tea into mugs.

**Cinnamon**
antibacterial, anti-inflammatory, antiviral, cough suppressant
**Cardamom**
antibacterial, anti-inflammatory, antipyretic, cough suppressant
**Ginger**
analgesic, antibacterial, anti-inflammatory
**Saffron**
antibacterial, anti-inflammatory, cough suppressant

# Feel-better Mint and Saffron Tea

**Serves 2**

From as far back as classical antiquity, saffron has been used to alleviate depression. Clinical studies conducted by Herbresearch at Tussenhausen have confirmed the anti-depressant effects of this precious spice. Saffron therefore has the potential to make a major contribution to herbal medicine.

**1 green tea bag**
**½ teaspoon saffron**
**a handful of fresh mint leaves**
**clear honey, to taste**

Place the tea bag and saffron in a saucepan. Add 2 mugs (600ml) cold water to the pan, and bring to the boil. Reduce to a low heat, cover and simmer gently for 10 minutes.

Place the mint leaves in the mugs. Remove the pan from the heat. Discard the tea bag and pour the tea and saffron mixture into the mugs, over the mint leaves. Add honey to taste.

**Saffron**
antidepressant
**Mint**
antidepressant

# Antihistamine Tea

**Serves 2**

Research into the treatment of allergies, by Humboldt University in Berlin, concluded that nigella seed oil can play a useful role in the management of conditions such as allergic rhinitis, bronchial asthma and atopic eczema.

**1 black tea bag**
**1 tablespoon nigella seeds**
**a handful of fresh mint leaves**
**clear honey, to taste**

Place the tea bag and nigella seeds in a saucepan. Add 2 mugs (600ml) cold water to the pan, and bring to the boil. Reduce to a low heat, cover and simmer gently for 10 minutes.

Place the mint leaves in the mugs. Remove the pan from the heat. Discard the tea bag, and strain the tea into the mugs, over the mint leaves. Add honey to taste.

**Nigella**
antihistamine, anti-inflammatory
**Mint**
antihistamine

# Pain-relief Tea

**Serves 2**

Research into the treatment of severe period pain, by Kerman University of Medical Science in Iran, found that fennel was more effective than nonsteroidal anti-inflammatory drugs (NSAIDs).

**3 black tea bags**
**1 tablespoon fennel seeds**
**1 stick of cinnamon**
**5 green cardamom pods, lightly crushed**
**1 teaspoon caraway seeds**
**a few cloves**
**a large pinch of ground ginger**
**a large pinch of black pepper**
**milk and sugar, to taste**

Place the tea bags, fennel seeds, cinnamon stick, cardamoms, caraway seeds, cloves, ginger and pepper in a saucepan. Add 3 mugs (900ml) cold water to the pan, and bring to the boil. Reduce to a low heat, cover and simmer gently for 10 minutes.

Stir in milk and sugar to taste. Continue to cook for 2 minutes, uncovered. Remove the pan from the heat. Discard the tea bags and strain the tea into mugs.

**Fennel**
analgesic, anti-inflammatory
**Cinnamon**
anti-inflammatory
**Cardamom**
anti-inflammatory
**Caraway**
analgesic, anti-inflammatory

**Clove**
analgesic, anti-inflammatory
**Ginger**
analgesic, anti-inflammatory

# Anti-flatulence and Anti-nausea Tea

**Serves 3**

Spices can come to the rescue in preventing and relieving flatulence. Research at the Central Food and Technological Research Institute at Mysore has shown how they can stimulate the production not only of bile but also of enzymes – both essential players in the digestive process. This tea also contains mint, which together with caraway, combats nausea.

**2 handfuls of fresh mint leaves**
**1 black tea bag**
**2 teaspoons fennel seeds**
**1 teaspoon caraway seeds**
**6cm piece of fresh root ginger, peeled**
**clear honey, to taste**

Divide the mint leaves equally between 3 mugs and set aside. Place the tea bag, fennel seeds, caraway seeds and ginger in a saucepan. Add 3 mugs (900ml) cold water to the pan, and bring to the boil. Reduce to a low heat, cover and simmer gently for 10 minutes.

Remove the pan from the heat. Discard the tea bag and strain the tea into the mugs, over the mint leaves. Add honey to taste.

**Mint**
anti-emetic
**Fennel**
anti-flatulent, anti-inflammatory, carminative, digestive
**Caraway**
anti-emetic, anti-inflammatory, digestive
**Ginger**
antibacterial, anti-emetic, anti-flatulent, anti-inflammatory, carminative, digestive

# Index

# Index

# Index

Left: Wholegrain Spelt and Seaweed Loaf, page 163
This page: Five-spice Chicken and Avocado on Wholegrain Toast, page 90

# Acknowledgements

I am truly fortunate in that I get to create concepts and share them with the world. Although my life is not always easy, there are people out there I can connect with, which means that I live each day with a great sense of accomplishment. So, foremost, I would like to thank my readers who give me reason to keep on dreaming.

At times the journey gets a bit choppy and there is one person who has stood by my side, through thick and thin, and that is my PR guru, Jon Kirk. A true gentleman.

A huge thank you to Nadia Ali for accommodating my absence while I wrote this book. You rock. Gratitude to Humara Qayyum, Justin Chen and Ghousia Ali for giving me space to grow.

Angels do exist here on earth. I have stumbled across two recently, who go by the names of Nigel Barden and Rebecca Pike.

A massive thumbs up to Sarah Stacey and Victoria Woodhall – two ladies that will inspire me always.

I would also like to recognise Jarek Filipowicz, for being my motivation and rock throughout the busiest period of my life to date.

To my mother, who has accommodated my various incarnations since birth, and who recently took on a purchasing officer's role, to keep the book moving along at light speed. I love you.

Thank you, Matt Inwood and Lara Holmes, for pulling off another beautiful book. A huge hug to my food stylist, Kate Calder, who delivered the book concept as intended and with a good pinch of her very own grace. For making the editing process as painless as possible I would like to give my editor, Diana Artley, a very special mention.

Of course, without my agent, Andrew Lownie, none of this would be at all possible.

I would like to say a heartfelt thank you to the rest of my supporters, who include Meg Avent, Tizer Bailey, Sanjeev Bhaskar MBE, Jon Croft, Chris Evans, Freddy Gangemi, Alice Gibbs, TRH The Duke and Duchess of Gloucester, Anthony Harvison, Ching-He Huang, Siyar Kaya, Rowan Morrice-Evans, Meera Syal MBE, Deborah Sass, Eleanor Weil, Dame Vivienne Westwood and Giles Whitman. If I have left anyone out, I owe you a drink!

For my spectacle frames, seen here in the book, I want to credit SpecSuperstore – look no further for the most stupendous selection of designer frames.

Last, but not least, I would like to honour Simon Mayo, a fan who also happens to be my biggest critic. I hope you like this one.